The Great Explainer

The Story of Richard Feynman

$\dot{z} = -p$
$\frac{dy}{dx}$
$\int \cos x \, dx = \sin$
$= q$
$= p(x)y$
$\iint \text{rot}\, U \, d$
$\cot \vec{5} = \nabla \times \vec{5}$
$\vec{5} = 0$
$\iint U \, d\vec{5} = \iiint \nabla U \, dV$
$\sin^2 \alpha + \cos^2 \alpha = 1$
$8/g = 0, \text{(8)}$
$\frac{dy}{dx} =$
$y^2 = (x-y)(x+y)$
$F(x \, y \, y')$
$P(x,y) \, dx +$
$\alpha + \beta + \gamma = \pi$

Profiles in Science

Tycho Brahe	**Galileo Galilei**
Robert Boyle	**Edmond Halley**
Nicholas Copernicus	**Ibn al-Haytham**
Marie Curie	**Caroline Herschel**
Charles Darwin	**Johannes Kepler**
Thomas Edison	**Antoine Lavoisier**
Michael Faraday	**Isaac Newton**
Rosalind Franklin	**Nikola Tesla**
Richard Feynman	

The Great Explainer

The Story of Richard Feynman

Harry LeVine, III

MORGAN REYNOLDS
PUBLISHING

GREENSBORO, NORTH CAROLINA

Morgan Reynolds Publishing
620 South Elm Street, Suite 223
Greensboro, NC 27406
www.morganreynolds.com
1-800-535-1504

Printed and bound in the United States.

First printing

1 3 5 7 9 8 6 4 2

Library of Congress Cataloging-in-Publication Data

LeVine, Harry, 1949-
   The great explainer : the story of Richard Feynman / by Harry
LeVine, III. — 1st ed.
      p. cm. — (Profiles in science)
   Includes bibliographical references and index.
   ISBN 978-1-59935-113-1
   1. Feynman, Richard Phillips—Juvenile literature.
2. Physicists—United States—Biography—Juvenile literature.
3. Physicists—United States—Intellectual life—20th
century—Juvenile literature. I. Title.
   QC16.F49L48 2009
   530.092—dc22
   [B]
                                        2009006677

To Melissa for her patience in giving me the time and space to research and write the story of this amazing physicist and curious character.

Table of Contents

Physicist Richard Feynman explains a scientific principle during a hearing into the space shuttle *Challenger* explosion, 1986. During an investigation Feynman found that unexpected cold temperatures had affected a critical gasket, causing the shuttle's destruction.

CHAPTER ONE

Far Rockaway

When the *Challenger* space shuttle exploded on January 28, 1986, a presidential commission of specially chosen scientists and researchers was tasked with finding out what happened. On the commission was a physicist from the California Institute of Technology (Caltech) named Richard Feynman. Feynman had joined the commission grudgingly; before accepting, he told his wife Gweneth, "I'm going to commit suicide for six months. I won't be able to do any work with this physics problem I've been having fun with; I'm going to do nothing but work on the Shuttle for six months." With the same intensity he focused on his physics, Feynman was determined to sift through the technical details of the complicated machine until he uncovered what had caused the disaster.

The commission followed a carefully orchestrated agenda, which Feynman felt would yield little new information. His approach was to go directly to the source and create his own picture from the raw data. This was in sharp contrast to the political maneuvering and bureaucracy of Washington. Still, Feynman, through his single-minded determination, was able to focus solely on the science of the problem, and ultimately played a key role in determining what had gone wrong with the *Challenger*. As he had his whole life, Feynman would successfully explain complicated science and use it to solve a problem.

Richard Phillips Feynman was born on May 11, 1918, in the borough of Manhattan in New York City. "If it's a boy he'll be a scientist," Richard's father Melville had said while his wife Lucille was pregnant with their first child. Melville's words proved true: Richard would become one of the most renowned physicists of the twentieth century.

Melville Feynman arrived in the United States at the age of five in 1895 with his parents, Lithuanian Jews from Minsk in Byelorussia. The family settled in Patchogue, Long Island. Melville wanted to be a doctor but family finances forced him to drop out of a homeopathic medicine program into a series of occupations including shirt manufacturing, dry cleaning, real estate, and uniform sales, ultimately becoming a sales manager for the Wender & Goldstein Company. In 1917, he married Lucille Phillips, the daughter of Polish Jews who escaped the Russian pogroms. The Phillips family had built a successful hat-making business in New York City. Although Melville never finished his medical training, he absorbed a great deal of knowledge and worked to pass his curiosity and passion for understanding the world on to his first son, Richard.

Richard Feynman, called Ritty by his family, grew up in a big two-story house with a large garden at 14 New Broadway in the rural resort village of Far Rockaway in Queens County, less than a mile from the beach on the southern shore of Long Island, a summer refuge for the professionals of New York City.

Ritty enjoyed a childhood typical for middle-class Jewish families. While the Feynmans were not rich, there was always enough food, new clothes when needed, and a new car, usually an Oldsmobile, every year. A woman came in several days a week to

The Feynman family lived near the beach in Far Rockaway, a neighborhood within the New York City borough of Queens. During the 1920s and 1930s, Far Rockaway was home to many Jewish and Eastern European immigrants.

do cleaning and laundry. When Ritty was five a baby brother was born, but he only lived for a month. Although they never talked about it, his normally cheerful mother became very quiet and cried easily. It took her several years to recover from the loss. In 1928, when Ritty was nine years old, his sister Joan was born.

The next year, in October, 1929 speculation by investors brought on a major stock market crash. This triggered an economic downturn which joined the world-wide Great Depression, during which nearly one-third of U.S. workers were unemployed. People had to scramble to make a living any way that they could. To save money, the Feynmans and the Lewines, Lucille's sister Pearl's family, shared the Far Rockaway house willed to the Phillips daughters by their father. The close quarters turned out to be fortunate for Ritty because it gave him ready-made playmates in his cousins, Robert, who was three years older, and Frances, a girl three years younger.

Ritty learned to walk early, but he worried his parents by not talking until he was nearly two years old. After that, he was unstoppably talkative. Melville played with his son constantly, helping him discover new things. When Ritty was a baby they made up a game arranging patterns with piles of colored tiles left over from when Melville sold bathroom tiles. When the boy was older he and his father would go for long walks around the mostly rural Far Rockaway. During summer vacations in the cool shade of the Catskill Mountains they wandered through the woods and along the streams.

Melville taught Ritty to notice little things around him and encouraged him to come up with his own explanation of how something might have happened. They talked about how things worked, how birds flew, how a gouge was made in that boulder, and how the ocean tides rose and fell. If you looked at anything closely enough, his father said, there would always be something interesting. During trips into New York City, they visited the Museum of Natural History and the dinosaur collection.

Whatever they did, Melville always emphasized the difference between simply knowing the name of something and actually knowing something and being able to explain what was happening. This attitude made a lasting impression on the young boy.

Melville also taught Ritty a healthy contempt for accepted respectability and authority. In the uniform business he had had plenty of experience with people who dressed up but had no substance. He held the same attitude towards knowledge and told his son, "Mind the reasoning alone, never mind the name of the man who said it."

Unemployed men wait for work at the New York City docks, 1934. To save money during the Great Depression, the Feynmans shared their home in Far Rockaway with relatives.

While Melville was serious about understanding the world around him, Ritty's mother was more light-hearted. She enjoyed jokes and tried to ease the matter-of-fact way in which Ritty approached life. She managed to instill in him a minimum of the social graces, although he never accepted etiquette that struck him as being false. She was also a great storyteller, a talent that Ritty inherited in full measure.

Melville read to Ritty and his sister Joan from the 1914 edition of the *Encyclopedia Britannica,* often in place of bedtime stories. Melville insisted that his children be able to practically explain whatever he taught them. A story remembered by Feynman was that a Tyrannosaurus stood twenty-five feet high and its head was six feet across. That meant it could look in their second story window but its head wouldn't fit inside. After he learned to read, Ritty pored over the science and nature sections of that encyclopedia.

One of the few other places in Far Rockaway that Ritty could go to learn more about science was the library, although they had few books on science. He was disappointed that the books written for children were too simple for him to learn much. One adult series that he enjoyed was *Mathematics for Self Study.* The librarian let him borrow the calculus book only when he said he was getting it for his father.

Neither Melville nor Lucille Feynman made the slightest attempt to develop Joan's interest in science. For all of his non-conventional thinking, and reading of the *Britannica* to both children, it simply never occurred to Melville that a girl would want to be a scientist. In the 1920s and 1930s, the prevailing opinion was that women were not able to be scientists. Joan's mother told her that women's brains were not up to doing science, even though Marie Curie had won the Nobel Prize in 1903 for discovering radium.

Ritty had no such prejudices. He thought that science was so interesting that everyone should want to do it. At age twelve, he was sometimes responsible for his three-year-old sister's care. For her amusement as well as his own he decided to teach her about numbers. He taught Joan how to add numbers together, rewarding correct answers by allowing her to pull his hair. In a small laboratory he had set up in a wooden crate in his bedroom, wired with switches and lights, she became his helper, earning four cents a week.

One night when Joan was four, Ritty got permission from his parents to wake her up, telling her that he had something wonderful to show her. They walked hand in hand onto the town golf course where Ritty pointed out the shimmering strands of the ghostly aurora borealis. Years later when she was thirteen, Ritty gave her a used college level astronomy text when he came back on break from graduate school at Princeton University. Ignoring her protests that it was too hard he said, "You start at the beginning and you read as far as you can, until you get lost. Then you start at the beginning again, and you keep working at it until you can understand the whole book."

After he went back to school she tried his suggestion. Eventually she came to a page with a spectrum of the different colors of light from a star. In the credits was the name of a woman astronomer, Cecilia Payne-Gaposhkin. At that point Joan knew that she could take her own interest in science seriously. She went on to earn her own Ph.D. in solid state physics and did aurora research.

Ritty's science interest developed rapidly. With his parents' blessing he built a small laboratory in the basement where he produced strange sounds and smells testing chemicals and developing photographs. His mother, when her bridge partners worried that he might blow up the house, said that it was worth the risk.

Ritty found that he learned much more from reading the *Britannica* and working on his own than from the once-day-a-week elementary school science class. Later he claimed that all he remembered from that class was that 39.37 inches = 1 meter. He taught himself arithmetic and algebra by inventing problems about the special properties of certain numbers and coming up with his own ways of solving them. He discovered later that the Babylonians and the Greeks had solved the same problems millennia earlier, but Ritty didn't care about that. They were his puzzles and he had figured them out himself. He impressed his cousin Robert's algebra tutor with his curiosity. The tutor encouraged Ritty to keep discovering things on his own.

By the fifth grade Ritty was already known as a scientific whiz kid. He helped seventh graders with their science and they kept the schoolyard bullies away from him. Sports held no interest for him. He was terrified walking by a ball field, worried that if a ball landed near him he wouldn't be able to throw it back. He had few interests or hobbies outside of science, but avoided the nerd stereotype with his spirit of adventure, ready wit, good looks, and determination to be part of the crowd. His early interest in science fiction faded as he realized that it was not very scientific. He stopped attending religion classes at the local temple when he was twelve because he didn't believe in miracles.

There were no true science role models in Far Rockaway, just as there were few science books in the public library. Dr. Marx, the family dentist, was as close as Ritty could get to a real scientist. The dentist answered what science questions he could and then connected the boy with another patient, William LeSeur, who taught English and filled in teaching general science at Far Rockaway High School. Ritty bicycled to the high school laboratory after grade school to help clean up, talk science, and do experiments. It was during these late afternoon sessions that he made an early impression on the high school chemistry teacher Joseph Johnson and the head of the science department, Dr. Edwin Barnes.

Ritty did experiments with a chemistry set his father had given him for his birthday and kept detailed notes of his observations. One day some neighborhood boys dumped all of his chemicals onto the sidewalk and threw a lighted match onto the bubbling mass to see if it would explode. Nothing happened. Ritty was angry about the destruction, and puzzled why anyone would be so silly. For him scientific things were to be handled carefully and in an organized way. The pleasure for him was in planning an experiment and observing the results.

As he got older, Ritty began to concentrate on experiments with radios and electricity. He made a microphone out of a speaker and strung wires around the house so that he could broadcast messages. A car battery powered his experiments, such as a burglar alarm that his parents set off coming home from a night out.

Ritty also learned how appliances and radios worked. He listened through the headphones of his homemade crystal radio set at night to the faint signals carrying music, news, and radio plays from as far away as Waco, Texas. From junk piles and rummage sales he picked up broken radios, cannibalized any usable parts, and constructed working radios which he sold to get better equipment. Pretty soon he was fixing neighbor's radios. His reputation spread.

One day he got a call for a repair and raced his bike across town at top speed to look at the problem. His customer was dismayed at how young the repairman was, but since Ritty was charging less than adults he let him go ahead. As the radio warmed up, a few scattered pops and hisses crescendoed into a steady roar. Ritty tried adjusting some of the connections but to no avail and shut it off. When the man impatiently asked him what he was doing Ritty replied that he was thinking, and contemplated the problem in silence. Without saying anything, he reached out and swapped the positions of the two identical amplifier tubes in the simple radio, then turned it back on. The crystal clear strains of a popular song greeted

Radio was an exciting new technology when Ritty was growing up. The first commercial radio station, KDKA in Pittsburgh, began broadcasting in November 1920. Ritty profited from his understanding of how radios work by selling his services as a repairman.

them in place of the deafening static. The man stared at him, incredulous, and paid Ritty his fee. From then on Ritty had a reputation: "He fixes radios by *thinking*." To Ritty it had simply been an amusing puzzle that he had solved with his knowledge of how radios work.

In addition to his radio repair work, Ritty had a series of odd jobs, like many of his schoolmates. He painted fences and walls and delivered printed handbill advertisements. He was fortunate that he could use his earnings to buy the odds and ends of chemicals, switches, and electrical components he needed for his laboratory. Many of his friends' earnings were needed to help support their families.

In the fall of 1931 at age thirteen and a half, Ritty entered ninth grade. He was looking forward to moving on to high school and the mathematical and scientific challenges that he expected to find there.

CHAPTER TWO

Budding Physicist

In high school, mathematics became Ritty's passion. As far back as the seventh and eighth grades, his facility with mathematics and his personal working style were apparent. Bored with the rote classwork, he taught himself algebra as an amusing puzzle, stimulated by eavesdropping on a math tutor working with his cousin Robert. He rarely did anything by the usual rules, but managed through intuitive reasoning to get the right answer. He worked out his own ways of solving simultaneous and linear equations.

To fuel Ritty's mathematical appetite and because the local library had few science books, he and his father made the twenty-mile trip on the Long Island Railway into New York City to Macy's Department Store to purchase a copy of *Calculus Made Easy*. When his father became confused trying to read the first chapter of the book, Ritty was shocked. He thought the chapter was easy.

With his friend Leonard Mautner, Ritty worked out most of the rules of Euclidean geometry entirely his own way one summer. With the knowledge of the sine of 5 degrees, he worked out a table for sines, cosines, and tangents of all angles using addition and a series of half-angle formulas he had derived for himself. He didn't care that this had been done before; he enjoyed the puzzle.

Ritty encountered his first difficulty with mathematics in high school solid geometry, studying three-dimensional objects such as spheres instead of circles. The diagrams of crisscrossing lines on the classroom chalkboard looked like utter chaos to him. "It was my only experience of how it [mathematics] must feel to the ordinary human being," he later said. He finally realized that the flat two-dimensional drawings on the chalk board were meant to represent three dimensional images. Then he could visualize everything again and solid geometry became easy. Whenever he saw a form such as a stream of water flowing from a faucet, he would try to work out the mathematical description of the shape.

Ritty appeared headed for a career as a mathematician, but he was more drawn to using mathematics to answer interesting, real world questions. He decided that "mathematics and science were of one piece" after fiddling with the formulas in *The Boy Electrician,* a book he found in the public library. The simple equations made a connection between the electricity and mathematical calculation.

During his senior year of high school in 1934, Abram Bader arrived to teach honors physics. Bader had been a graduate student of the physicist Isidor Rabi at Columbia, but lacking the finances to complete his thesis, turned to teaching. Bader quickly realized that Richard Feynman was the top student, but he also presented a challenge. Pulling Ritty out of class once for being disruptive, Bader astutely realized the problem was boredom with the course material. He gave Ritty his college *Advanced Calculus* book, complete with his notes in the margins of sections he did not understand, and told him to sit in the back of the class and study the book. Feynman returned the book in less than a month and proceeded to explain the answers to Bader's questions. Ritty added advanced vector analysis from reading his cousin's tutor's Columbia University mathematics thesis.

One afternoon after a class during which Ritty had been disruptive, he and Bader were alone in the laboratory. Bader went to the board and drew a series of paths that an object could follow starting at point A when thrown at a given speed and ending at point B. He asked Ritty how to calculate which path would take the least amount of time. He proceeded to tell Ritty about a different way of expressing physical laws of motion that would determine the trajectory that would be the most efficient. It was called the Principle of Least Action in which all possible pathways were considered, but it turned out that objects always followed the pathway of least resistance.

Calculations using the Principle of Least Action would give the same results for physics problems as the traditional differential equations, but it avoided certain kinds of mathematical difficulties. It provided an intuitive method which also turned out to be mathematically correct. The Principle of Least Action became the model Ritty would use when he was stuck on a new problem.

Aside from mathematics, Ritty's main interest during high school was in meeting girls. Ritty's attention centered on one girl in particular. The summer he entered high school, he had been captivated by a beautiful girl combing out her long dark hair after an afternoon of swimming on the Far Rockaway beach. Her name was Arline Greenbaum. He found excuses to see her, even joining the Art Club, despite a lack of aptitude for anything artistic, because Arline was in it. Even though Ritty and Arline seemed to be opposites, one scientifically gifted and logical to the point of obsession, and the other artistic and socially involved, they grew close.

In May of 1935, his senior year, Ritty placed first in the Pi Mu Epsilon New York City-wide math contest for all public and private high schools. His high school yearbook records that his classmates voted Ritty Mad Genius. At graduation from Far Rockaway High School later that spring, Ritty won the class prizes in math, physics, and chemistry. To his amusement, he also won the prize in his worst subject, English.

Despite growing up during the economic hardships of the Depression, Ritty was never career-minded in high school. He did not know, nor did he care, about where the best opportunities lay. He simply loved the challenge of mathematics. The wishes of his father and mother that he go to college were reinforced by Dr. Augsberry, the chairman of the Far Rockaway High School Department of Mathematics. At graduation, he impressed on Lucille Feynman the importance of Ritty having the chance to reach his potential in college.

Ritty took the entrance examination for Columbia University, which cost fifteen dollars, but was rejected because Columbia's Jewish admittance quota had been exceeded for that year. He was bothered less by the religious quota at Columbia and at other schools—that was the way things were—than by the waste of the fifteen dollars.

Ritty was accepted to the Massachusetts Institute of Technology (MIT) in Cambridge, Massachusetts, and was awarded a partial hundred dollar a year scholarship. MIT was well known for its rigorous science and engineering programs, but less so for an aggressive program of socialization. This included a compulsory Tea for all freshmen to provide instruction in the art of making polite conversation and other basic social graces. Fraternities were segregated by religion, as elsewhere, so Feynman joined Phi Beta Delta, one of two Jewish fraternities on campus. There he found intellectual stimulation with the house's emphasis on scholarship.

Feynman took the challenging math, physics, and engineering coursework in stride. It was what he had signed up for, but he balked at the requirements for literature, art, music, religion, and philosophy. MIT subscribed to the European fashion of the educationally well-rounded scientist or engineer. He went to great lengths to avoid as much of the humanities coursework as possible, only occasionally complying with his fraternity brothers' suggestions to complete assignments so that he wouldn't wreck the fraternity's grade point average.

Feynman had entered MIT attracted by its pure mathematics, but he wanted to use the math to solve interesting problems. When he asked the math department's chairman what mathematics was good for, he was told that if he had to ask, then he was in the wrong field. Feynman instead focused on physics. The Physics Department chairman, John C. Slater, was equally pragmatic. He preached that theories must make reasonably good predictions of experimental outcomes. His textbook was revolutionary for the time, unifying fields of physics which normally were taught separately with modern atomic theory.

As advanced as atomic theory was in 1935, American universities still had not incorporated the newest physical theory, quantum mechanics, which promised to explain events at the level of the constituents of the atom. In the years between 1925 and 1927, a complete revolution in physics occurred in Germany. The idea of light as an electromagnetic wave and a particle, a quantum, was first proposed by Max Planck in 1900 to explain the emission of light from heated objects, like a red hot piece of iron. A similar conclusion was reached by Albert Einstein in 1905 to explain the generation of an electric current by light falling on certain metals, for which he won his Nobel Prize.

To deal with the apparent contradictions between particles and waves, in 1925 Werner Heisenberg formulated quantum mechanics to construct a theory incorporating the concept of an inherent uncertainty in knowledge about a particle. His method built on experimentally measured quantities rather than trying to derive a theory from an assumed model of the atom. Paul

The Massachusetts Institute of Technology (MIT) was founded in 1861 by William Barton Rogers, a noted nineteenth-century American scientist and educator. MIT's curriculum focused on scientific and technological research, areas that Rogers felt would help the United States compete during the ongoing Industrial Revolution.

Dirac showed in 1927 that the wave and particle interpretations were equivalent. He combined the mathematics of probabilities introduced by Erwin Schrödinger with Heisenberg's uncertainty principle into an equation that predicted experimental results with amazing precision. *Physical Review*, the main publication for physicists, carried articles using the new quantum mechanics but there was no textbook available and no courses on this new way of viewing the atomic world.

In the spring of 1936, Feynman and another precocious sophomore, T. A. Welton, began a program to teach themselves quantum mechanics. They kept a notebook in which they wrote their derivations and their musings about what they didn't understand. When they went home over the summer, they mailed the notebook back and forth, taking turns deriving and questioning each other.

Feynman and Welton took a graduate course as juniors on the theory of nuclear structure which centered on a series of three long papers written by a young German physicist at Cornell named Hans Bethe who had escaped from Hitler's Germany in 1933. Feynman found them particularly interesting. He and Welton were at the forefront of physics, learning things for which the textbooks had not yet been written.

In the early decades of the twentieth century, Albert Einstein (1879–1955) and Max Planck (1858–1947) developed ground-breaking theories about the nature and properties of atoms, the basic building blocks of the universe. Their work became the basis for a new branch of physics, known as quantum mechanics.

Feynman did a series of projects for professors in the department, and succeeded in publishing his first paper in *Physical Review* with Dr. Manuel S. Vallarta on the scattering of cosmic rays by galaxies. In his spare time, Feynman played games translating formulas into physical situations so that he could have an intuitive feeling for what the equations meant.

Feynman took on a senior thesis project with the Physics Department chairman Slater. The original question, about why quartz expands so little when heated, took an unanticipated direction, and resulted in a fundamental discovery about forces acting within and between molecules. Feynman devised a simple computational method to calculate the force law between molecules which conjured up a physically appealing picture of the molecular situation. Combined with work from another physicist, the Feynman-Hellman force theorem became a standard tool in solid state physics. Feynman later dismissed it as obvious and something that he should have written in "half a line."

Graduate school was clearly the next step for Feynman. When he told his advisor he wanted to continue on at MIT, Slater asked him, "Why do you want to go to MIT?" Feynman answered, "Because it's the best school in the country for science and engineering." Slater responded, "That's why you have to go to another school for your graduate work." Feynman chose Princeton, because he had noticed many papers in the *Physical Review* from there.

Slater and the faculty at MIT pushed strongly for Feynman's acceptance but several things stood in his way: Feynman's cavalier attitude toward non-science coursework, his low scores on graduate exams in subjects other than science, and his Jewish background. The best physics and math scores the Princeton admissions committee had ever seen were balanced against the lowest scores they had ever seen in history, literature, and fine arts. A thornier issue was the strict limit on the number of Jews allowed into the program. A number of handwritten postscripts on his recommendations assured the admissions committee that Feynman neither looked nor acted Jewish. The admissions committee finally relented, and after a summer job in Boston with the Chrysler Corporation measuring the friction on surfaces polished by a new method, Feynman began his graduate work at Princeton in the fall of 1939.

At the Princeton Graduate College, students in all of the disciplines lived and ate together in the same building. Feynman argued with the philosophers and listened to the biologists, but spent most of his free time discussing mathematics. He found that the lack of course requirements and the focus on scholarly research fitted his temperament perfectly. Other than passing a set of preliminary exams and an oral defense of his thesis work, he and his advisor, the newly arrived John A. Wheeler, would fashion his course of study.

Wheeler soon discovered Feynman's special talents and their relationship became more that of colleagues than mentor-student. Feynman earned his graduate assistant stipend of fifteen dollars a week, working on problems posed by Wheeler, but he finished them so quickly that he had ample time to explore his own ideas. He wanted to decipher the unsolved problems of physics. He took to heart the last sentence in Dirac's 1935 textbook *Principles of Quantum Mechanics*, "It seems that some essentially new physical ideas are here needed."

The need to reformulate principles in his own terms was Feynman's trademark. His Ph.D. thesis was an example. He and Wheeler were trying to explain the interaction between two separated electrons. The current methods used fields and waves, the currency of the new quantum mechanics, but they couldn't account for the interaction of an electron with itself. The mathematics of the solution failed close to the electron.

Colored postcard from the early twentieth century showing the library at Princeton University. Feynman attended the graduate college at Princeton from September 1939 to June 1942.

Feynman ended up taking an approach based on the path integral. It used a mathematical formalism called a Lagrangian which he manipulated so that it described classical and quantum mechanics—light as waves and particles—equally well.

Life was not entirely physics. Feynman and Arline Greenbaum had continued to draw closer to one another. She spent many weekends in Boston while he was at MIT. Shortly after he moved to Princeton they had agreed to marry, but Feynman's scholarships would have been revoked if he married. In addition, a strange lump on Arline's neck and her constant tiredness were diagnosed as tuberculosis, which at the time was an incurable, lethal disease. Feynman's parents tried to talk him out of marrying Arline, concerned for his career and worried he would contract the disease. Their arguments had no effect, but he did need his scholarship, so he and Arline agreed to wait until he graduated.

War had enveloped Europe in the autumn of 1939 and it was clear that it would only be a matter of time before the United States became involved. After listening to a sobering speech at Princeton by a visiting general, Feynman felt that he ought to do something for the war effort. He gave up a summer job at Bell Laboratories to work at the Frankfort Arsenal in Philadelphia on a mechanical director device that would track and point an antiaircraft gun at attacking planes. He was so successful that the Army offered him a long term job to direct his own design team, but he was turned off by military bureaucracy and returned to Princeton in the Fall.

On December 8, 1941, after the Japanese attack on the U.S. naval fleet at Pearl Harbor, the U.S. declared war on Japan and Germany. Princeton suspended much of its academic degree work and asked graduate students to take up war-related projects. Feynman's advisor, Wheeler, left for Chicago to work on a secret project, later revealed to be the first atomic reactor. Later in December, Feynman was absorbed in writing his thesis when he was interrupted by faculty member Robert Wilson, who told him about a secret project to build an atomic bomb. A number of leading German atomic physicists had disappeared, and the U.S. government was worried that they were developing their own atomic weapon. Wilson wanted Feynman's help in building a bomb for the U.S.

Feynman assured Wilson that he would keep the secret, but he was busy and he didn't want to work under Army bureaucracy. After Wilson left, though, Feynman thought about the consequences of Germany having an atomic bomb and shoved his thesis paper into his desk drawer. He decided he would go to work on the building of the bomb.

CHAPTER THREE

Project Y— Los Alamos

Three months later, John Wheeler called from Chicago to tell Feynman that he should take this last chance to "write up what you have in the remaining weeks before you get into the situation in which I find myself." With this warning, Feynman pulled the scrap paper sheets on which he had scrawled a draft of his thesis from the desk drawer and requested a few weeks off from the uranium separation project, now part of the secret Manhattan Project, to finish writing. When he was done he had created the framework of a new theory of quantum electrodynamics. He then prepared to devote his energy to the atomic bomb project.

In June 1942, Feynman officially received his Ph.D. and on July 29, 1942, he and Arline Greenbaum were married by a justice of the peace on Staten Island in front of the bookkeeper and the accountant at the registry office. Their honeymoon was a ride on the Staten Island ferry back to the mainland. Arline was too ill for them to keep house together. They drove to Arline's new home, the Deborah Hospital in New Jersey, where he could visit her on weekends.

The Army Corps of Engineers' Madison Square office at 261 Fifth Avenue in New York City looked like any other office. There was no indication that the world's largest and most complicated military-industrial project originated from the Manhattan Engineering District, the code designation for the program. Although ground work such as the isotope separation feasibility that Feynman was working on had begun near the end of 1941, authorization for the development and construction of an atomic bomb didn't come until August 13, 1942.

To create a useable weapon in time to affect the outcome of the war, several approaches for critical processes in the project were tried at the same time. One of these was the difficult separation of kilogram quantities of the seven parts of fissionable uranium-235 from the 993 parts of contaminating uranium-238 by their 1.3 percent difference in mass. Robert Wilson's Princeton group was dismayed when gaseous diffusion rather than the isotron mass spectrometer process they had been working on was chosen for industrial scale production of U-235, now code named 25.

The Nobel Prize–winning Italian physicist Enrico Fermi (1901–1954) recognized that a nuclear reaction would unleash enormous amounts of energy. In 1942, Fermi directed a team that created the first self-sustaining nuclear reactor at the University of Chicago. He served as a consultant on the Manhattan Project.

While waiting for his section to be re-assigned, Wilson sent Feynman to Chicago to learn about Enrico Fermi's work with the first sustained chain reaction. This atomic reactor was literally a 'pile' of carefully interspersed pieces of uranium and specially purified graphite stacked under the squash courts at the University of Chicago. At the code-named Metallurgical Laboratory there, Feynman created a lasting impression by solving several calculation bottlenecks that had stymied their work. When he returned to Princeton, Wilson's group had already shifted to building radiological detection equipment.

The bomb project was taking shape under a thick blanket of security. Different parts of the project were not permitted to communicate except through certain individuals. General Leslie R. Groves, of the U.S. Army Corps of Engineers, who had supervised the building of the massive Pentagon military offices in Washington, D.C., and other large Corps projects, had selected J. Robert Oppenheimer from the University of California at Berkeley to lead the scientific part of the enterprise. Although some disapproved of Oppenheimer's selection because Oppenheimer's wife had been a member of the Communist Party, Groves stood by his choice. He believed that besides having the respect of the scientists, "Oppie" was the only one capable of managing the many different technical aspects of the project to produce a bomb in time to be of use in the war.

A desolate mesa outside of Santa Fe, New Mexico, was agreed on as a place where secret work of this magnitude and danger could be carried out. The site, at Los Alamos Ranch School for boys, was a place where scientists could gather and could exchange enough information to carry out their tasks, yet be controlled and isolated to maintain security.

Los Alamos was the hub for the research effort and the final assembly of the bomb. Bomb components, particularly the industrial scale production of U-235 and Pu-239 (code name

49), a fissionable isotope of the new element plutonium made by bombarding U-238 (code name 28) with neutrons in a nuclear reactor were prepared at separate sites. These materials and all other components funneled into the main development center at Los Alamos. That was where the bomb was designed, and components assembled and tested.

The key to the success of the scientific effort was Oppenheimer's attention to detail and his genius in obtaining the confidence, respect, and loyalty of the scientists. This was not an easy task because the organization and leadership of groups needed to be fluid as the project progressed. Many scientists with key skills who had fled Nazi Germany had to be incorporated along with some scientists from other nations. Complicating the issue was that the scientists were not military personnel who could be ordered about, although that option was suggested by General Groves and dismissed by Oppenheimer.

Feynman's loyalty to Oppenheimer and the project was sealed when Oppenheimer called him from Chicago to tell him that he had located a room in Presbyterian Sanatorium in Albuquerque for Arline, where Feynman could visit her on weekends. "It was the first time that I met him in such a personal way; he was a wonderful man."

Wilson's group had been told when booking their train tickets to leave from somewhere other than Princeton to disguise their movements. Feynman figured that meant he would be the only one leaving from there, so he and Arline left Princeton on the train on March 28, 1943, bound for Lamy, New Mexico. He settled her in the Sanatorium, then reported to a nondescript office in Santa Fe where the research team members were processed. After a thirty-five mile ride up the treacherous road cut into the mountainside he arrived in Los Alamos.

Feynman was assigned to the T Section (for Theoretical) headed by Hans Bethe, who had published the seminal papers Feynman and T. A. Welton had studied as juniors at MIT. He

General Leslie Groves (left) confers with J. Robert Oppenheimer, 1945. Groves (1896–1970) had overseen several large construction projects before being placed in charge of the U.S. Army's secret program to develop an atomic weapon. He chose Oppenheimer (1904–1967), a respected physicist and professor at the University of California at Berkeley, to serve as scientific director for the Manhattan Project.

was given the task of calculating the efficiency of a nuclear explosion. While Fermi had been able to calculate the amount of U-235 needed to obtain a continuous chain reaction (called criticality), they now needed to know the minimal amount of fissionable material for supercriticality—the runaway fission required to make a bomb. What made the calculation difficult was that none of this had ever been done before and there was almost no experimental data available.

Bethe began to value Feynman, though only age twenty-four, for his blunt criticism and penetrating insight. He appreciated that Feynman wanted to work on all of the problems, not just one. Bethe also recognized Feynman's originality and keen sense of practicality and made him Group Leader of T-4, Diffusion Problems, working on the critical mass issue. By age twenty-five, Feynman was head of a four-person team that

German-American scientist Hans Bethe (1906–2005), head of the Theoretical Division of the Manhattan Project, recognized Feynman's ability and soon placed him in charge of a research group.

included Welton. Their work would set the goals for production of fissionable material.

Feynman's group became proficient at approximations that were astonishingly accurate in predicting the experimental results that came trickling in from other groups. Feynman used a crude form of parallel processing to speed calculations by dividing up each problem into parts on color-coded cards and then employing teams of calculators, often the wives of the scientists using Marchant and Monroe mechanical calculators and crude electronic devices from IBM, to solve the separate parts which were combined in later steps to give the final result. He also devised a scheme that would trap errors so that they would not spread through the many steps of a calculation.

On weekends when Feynman visited Arline, he hitchhiked or borrowed a car to drive the hundred miles to Albuquerque. He did his best to inject some normalcy into their married life even though she wasn't able to leave the sanatorium. Like many young couples they spent hours talking about their future once the war was over, even as Arline wasted away day by day. They both realized that her tuberculosis was a death sentence but resolved to live the time they had to the fullest.

It wasn't possible to telephone, so they wrote almost daily letters. This caused a problem because wartime censorship was being enforced. The couple loved puzzles and for amusement would make up a code that the other had to figure out. Letters would arrive with sections blacked out or cut out by the censors. Feynman responded by tweaking the military censors with something that looked like a code. They were not in the mood for jokes, though. Anyone less critical to the project would have been thrown in the brig. Finally, Feynman agreed that he and Arline would send a copy of the code in their letter which the censors would use to read the note and then remove before sending it on.

Feynman often challenged the enforcement of arbitrary rules by uniformed Army guards, and had multiple brushes with Los Alamos security. It wasn't all for fun. Sometimes he pointed out serious flaws that could jeopardize the secret nature of the work. He noticed holes in the perimeter fencing that local construction contractors were using as shortcuts to jobsites in the complex. When the Army didn't respond to his reporting of the holes, he decided to show them how easy it was to evade detection. He entered through the main gate, showed his ID badge to get past the guards, crawled out through one of the holes and came back in through the main gate. After several rounds, the guards became suspicious and arrested Feynman. Hans Bethe had to bail him out.

Another time he demonstrated the ease of obtaining any information he wanted about the project. He deduced the combinations of document safes containing the bomb design, but instead of taking anything, he would leave an unsigned note saying what he had done and carefully lock the safes again.

Feynman's talent as a teacher was recognized early on at Los Alamos. He had the knack of being able to explain complex problems to any group of people, breaking it down without oversimplifying, to give them an intuitive sense of the issues. This proved valuable, as Feynman found that he could increase efficiency and cut down on errors if he explained the process of what a group was doing and why they did things a certain way. This was going against Army security policy, which demanded that the scientists only have as much information as was necessary to complete their individual tasks.

Late in the development of the bomb, potentially cata-strophic safety issues were discovered at the Project X site at Oak Ridge, Tennessee, where the U-235 for the bombs was being enriched. Feynman was delegated to explain to the man-agers what the diffusion plant was doing, how that would help the war effort, and how safety measures could avoid having too much U-235 in one place. Learning about the logic of the process motivated workers to improve their safety methods. Many people at the Oak Ridge plant believed that Feynman saved their lives by preventing an accident.

In May of 1945, Arline's father had come from New York to visit his daughter, a difficult and expensive trip in wartime. In June, he found that he could not stand to be with her any more. He called Feynman in Los Alamos to tell him that Arline was near her end. Instead of hitchhiking, Feynman borrowed his good friend Klaus Fuchs's blue Buick, managing despite a series of flat tires to get to Arline's bedside that evening. She was weak, only able to follow things with her eyes, and died a few hours later. He returned to the laboratory the next day. When people asked him how Arline was, he replied shortly, "She's dead. And how's the [computer] program going?" He didn't want to talk about the loss.

For several weeks Feynman threw himself into his work with renewed intensity. Hans Bethe sensed that he needed to enforce a break, and sent Feynman back to Far Rockaway for a rest. Feynman protested, but Bethe insisted. Back home, Feynman was finally forced to confront and accept Arline's death. She had been his first true love, "a love like no other that I know of."

It was also a difficult time because of the frosty relations between Feynman and his parents, particularly with his

Workers prepare a plutonium bomb for the Trinity bomb test in the New Mexico desert, July 1945.

mother. They had opposed his marriage to Arline on the grounds of her tuberculosis so vehemently that he stopped communicating with them and had not returned home for almost three years. He roamed the beaches of his childhood at Far Rockaway trying to regain his mental footing. Finally, a coded telegram from Bethe arrived announcing, "The baby is expected." He quickly traveled directly to Hans Bethe's house in Los Alamos.

A flat expanse of open desert named Jornada del Muerto (Journey of Death) near Alamogordo, New Mexico, had been selected as the test site for the plutonium implosion weapon, Trinity. The remoteness and prevailing wind conditions would sweep radioactive debris away from populated areas and the mountains would screen the activity from view.

On July 16, 1945, the bomb they had been working on was set off.

At 5:29 AM, before the dawn, the horizon flashed from semi-darkness to the brilliant white light of noon. A sheet of clouds materialized in the visible shock wave above the fireball, reflecting blue and orange from their undersides. Richard Feynman stood with a group of scientists watching as a mushroom-shaped cloud rose from the flatness of the desert, surrounded by the purple glow of air ionized by the intense radiation released in the fission event for the few microseconds before the device blew itself into oblivion. The boiling orange clouds were beginning to dim when a minute and a half later the sound of the explosion reached them.

This model of the implosion-type atomic bomb, code-named "Fat Man," is on display at the Bradbury Science Museum at Los Alamos National Laboratory. This weapon was similar in design to the device exploded at Alamogordo, New Mexico, on July 16, 1945.

No one spoke. Even at twenty miles distance they could feel the roar in their bones. Feynman disliked the dark welder's glasses issued for eye protection, reasoning that the glass of the Jeep windshield he was standing behind would block the ultraviolet light emitted by the atmosphere ionized by the extreme heat of the explosion.

Dawn of the atomic age: a brilliant fireball erupts at the successful Trinity test.

Enrico Fermi, who had overseen the building of the first atomic reactor in Chicago two years earlier, stood calmly apart from the rest, tearing bits off of a piece of paper and dropping them, watching them drift two and quarter meters in the blast wave to calculate the force of the explosion. Ten kilotons, he announced. There had been a betting pool on the explosive force calculated in tons of the high explosive TNT, with guesses ranging from a complete fizzle to twenty kilotons.

The explosion was heard from a distance of one hundred miles, the flash seen 180 miles away. To protect the secrecy of the test, the commanding officer of the Alamogordo Army Air Base issued a press release to local communities saying that "A remotely located ammunition magazine containing a considerable amount of high explosives and pyrotechnics exploded."

Celebration broke out among many of the scientists. Twenty-eight months of frenzied work by many thousands of people and more than $2 billion had paid off. But some were awed and sobered by the power that they had released. There had been no time to reflect on the consequences of their work. Robert Wilson was morose, saying "It's a terrible thing that we made."

(Left) The American B-29 bomber *Enola Gay* lands on Tinian, an island in the Marianas chain, after dropping the first atomic bomb on Hiroshima, August 6, 1945. (Opposite) This aerial view of Hiroshima shows the devastation wrought by the atomic bomb. The blast killed an estimated 120,000 Japanese immediately, with tens of thousands of others later dying from their injuries or from radiation poisoning.

Feynman celebrated their success, sitting on the back of a Jeep drumming on metal trash cans and partying. A huge project involving tens of thousands of people had created new elements and brought theory to practicality. He later wrote a letter to his mother about the test saying "Everything was perfect, except for the aim." He saw the weapon as a way to end the war quickly with minimal loss of Allied lives. Later, he was less enthusiastic about the use of the bomb.

Three weeks after Trinity, on August 6, 1945, a mushroom cloud erupted over the Japanese city of Hiroshima and three days after that a second bomb destroyed Nagasaki. Depending on the source, between 200,000 and 500,000 people were killed in the bombings, or from diseases related to the radiation given off by the explosion. The war ended on August 14, 1945.

With the war over, after two years of tireless work, the pressure was suddenly off. Los Alamos demobilized nearly as quickly as it had been formed. Some of the scientists found it hard to leave the isolated mesa, and stayed on with the Los Alamos laboratory which in the ensuing years became the main site for U.S. nuclear weapons development. Feynman was offered the chance by Edward Teller to stay and work on the "Super," the hydrogen bomb which was based on nuclear fusion and was hundreds of times more powerful than the

atomic bombs used on Japan. Feynman refused, saying that he had done what was needed when the U.S. was attacked but would do no more.

Feynman stood out, though, even among the great collection of scientists and engineers at Los Alamos, and he received many other offers. As early as October 1943, Hans Bethe had told Cornell University that he wanted to bring Feynman back with him to join the physics faculty after the war. Oppenheimer had tried to get Berkeley to make an offer to Feynman but it arrived too late. Although he received a number of other offers, Feynman accepted the Cornell appointment.

Feynman was the first Group Leader to leave Los Alamos. He only had to finish a few reports and to make final safety tours at the Hanford, Washington, plutonium production facility and the Oak Ridge uranium enrichment plant. He was walking down the street in Oak Ridge when he saw a pretty dress in a department store window and suddenly thought that Arline would surely like it. Then it hit him that Arline was dead and he broke down. They were the first tears he had shed for Arline since her death.

At the invitation of Hans Bethe, Feynman agreed to join the faculty at Cornell University in Ithaca, New York, in the fall of 1945. The Ivy League school was considered one of the top universities in the country. Pictured is a well-known Cornell landmark, the McGraw clock tower.

CHAPTER FOUR

Adrift–Epiphany

A few weeks before he began teaching at Cornell, Feynman tried to resolve the rift between him and his parents over Arline. His mother had been devastated by the coldness of their relationship since the marriage and had written him letter after letter trying to win him back. With Arline gone, he was finally ready to reconcile. His father, who did not often write letters, had written him, "The dreams I have often had in *my* youth for my own development, I see coming true in your career."

A few days later, on October 7, 1945, fifty-six year old Melville Feynman collapsed from a stroke and died the next day. At his father's interment at the Phillips mausoleum at Bayside Cemetery in Queens, Feynman refused to say the Kaddish, the Jewish mourner's prayer. He felt that it would be hypocritical since neither he nor his father believed in God. One of his life's rules was to be truthful, regardless of the consequences.

The two people closest to Richard Feynman had died within the last two years and he felt completely alone. On October 17 he sat down and wrote a letter.

"D'Arline, I adore you, sweetheart," it began. He explained that even though she wouldn't want it that way, his love for her was standing in the way of him loving someone else. He ended with:

> My darling wife, I do adore you.
> I love my wife. My wife is dead.
>   Rich.
> P.S. Please excuse my not mailing this—but
> I don't know your new address.

He sealed the letter and put it in a box where it remained, unopened, until after his death. He was finally able to accept that she was gone from his life and that he could begin anew. His new job at Cornell would provide the perfect opportunity to do so.

It was midnight on Halloween, 1945, when Feynman arrived in Ithaca, New York. He had ridden the train all the way from Albuquerque, New Mexico, stopping to give a talk at the University of Iowa in Ames. Troops returning from the war had created a housing shortage in Ithaca, so there were no hotel rooms or apartments to be had in town. After lugging his suitcase from hotel to hotel, Feynman found a taxi to take him up the hill and wandered about the lower Cornell campus. Around 2 AM he found an empty couch in the lobby of the Student Union, Willard Straight Hall, and slept there.

Feynman had decided that he wanted to teach students how to do physics the way he did physics. At Los Alamos he had become accustomed to explaining things and lecturing on a wide variety of topics, so he plunged into teaching with gusto.

Much to the initial dismay of senior faculty, he neglected standard course content to concentrate on working a large number of illustrative problems approached in innovative ways. Feynman tried to give the students practical skills. He wanted them to feel the real-life situation of doing physics in an area where the physicist did not have solid knowledge but needed to be able to get some kind of useful answer.

His exotic approach and talent as an entertaining lecturer soon attracted many of the junior faculty from his own and other departments on campus in addition to the students taking the course. At one time or another while at Cornell he taught all the theoretical courses on classical, statistical, and quantum mechanics as well as relativity, approaching each with his own style.

Although his teaching was going well, Feynman was less satisfied with his social life. He went to dances to try to fill some of the void left by Arline's death. The women refused to believe his stories about working on the atomic bomb or that he was a professor, thinking that he was just using a line on them. Eventually, he stopped talking about his war work and found a few dance partners, but they couldn't replace Arline.

Even more frustrating to Feynman was his inability to accomplish any significant research. At first he concentrated on preparing his lectures and his teaching responsibilities. He needed time to decompress from wartime demands and the fixation on creating a weapon. But when he tried to work he couldn't settle down. He would pick up a problem, work on it for a little while, and then drop it because he felt that it was unimportant. He was at the point in his career that he should be making his mark on physics. Instead, he felt paralyzed.

Feynman gave little evidence of this inner struggle. Even his close associates had no hint that Feynman was depressed. A former colleague of his at Los Alamos, with whom he now shared an office at Cornell said, "Feynman depressed is just a little more cheerful than any other person when he is exuberant."

Compounding his frustration were offers of prestigious positions at Berkeley, University of Pennsylvania, and even the home of Albert Einstein, the Princeton Institute for Advanced Study. Feynman felt he didn't deserve any of the positions. He dealt with this by deciding that he was not responsible for other people's impression of his abilities, and he wasn't going to feel

Robert R. Wilson (1914–2000) worked with Feynman at Princeton, on the Manhattan Project, and at Cornell University.

guilty for not living up to what other people expected of him. He turned down the offers. His former mentor, Robert R. Wilson, now head of the Cornell Newman Laboratory for Nuclear Studies, supported his position, telling him that he shouldn't worry about his lull in productivity or feel guilty. He should do whatever he felt happiest doing.

A few days later, Feynman had an epiphany. During lunch in a student cafeteria, someone tossed a plate bearing the Cornell seal into the air. He noticed that the plate was wobbling more rapidly than it was spinning. The motion of the university seal intrigued him and he couldn't help trying to work out the equation of its path using only Newton's law of motion. It was a simple problem. No one's life or the future of the world depended on its solution. It was just a fun puzzle. He ran to Hans Bethe's office and told him about his discovery. When Bethe asked him how that was important, Feynman replied that it had no importance, nor did he care. "That's all I'm going to do from now on: have fun!"

Resolving to have fun brought Feynman release from his self-imposed intellectual prison. He picked up on his old thesis problem which had been pushed to the back of his mind by Los Alamos and began to toy with it. One of the difficulties with applying his theory of summing the probabilities of all the possible paths a particle could take was that there was no analog of the quantum property of the electron described by the Dirac equation called spin.

He began his investigation by first creating the simplest possible model: in this case, a one-dimensional universe in which a particle could travel only on a line. It could move left or right, constantly at the speed of light. From this he constructed a two-dimensional diagram in which a particle could move both up and down and from side to side. He plotted position on the horizontal axis and time on the vertical axis. After some manipulations, he found that a mathematical property of his graph, called the phase in his path integral formulation, was equivalent to Dirac's spin on the electron. It was a "Eureka" moment, one that would define his career.

Feynman sensed a breakthrough and worked feverishly to try his new idea out on more complex systems. Many fundamental problems in quantum physics had remained unsolved since the late 1920s. The prevailing theory was unable to

During the 1920s and 1930s, the British theoretical physicist Paul Dirac (1902–1984) helped to develop the field of quantum mechanics. In 1928 Dirac predicted the existence of atomic-level antiparticles, such as the positron, which later experiments proved to exist. For his contributions to atomic theory, Dirac shared the 1933 Nobel Prize in Physics.

account for new highly accurate measurements of properties of the electron. The harder theorists pushed their equations for detail, the more absurd the predictions became. At a conference on the future of nuclear science, Feynman had remarked, "We need an intuitive leap at the mathematical formalism, such as we had in the Dirac electron theory. We need a stroke of genius."

A series of three small conferences on the foundations of quantum physics was organized by the National Academy of Sciences. The first, "Problems of Quantum Mechanics and the Electron," was held June 2-4, 1947, at the Ram's Head Inn at the tip of Long Island. Twenty-four of the country's top theoretical quantum physicists, including twenty-nine year-old Richard Feynman, gathered at what became known as the Shelter Island Conference.

A talk by Willis Lamb on the hydrogen atom and another by Isidor Rabi on deuterium and more complex atoms presented new, highly accurate experimental measurements of an unexpected separation of energy levels within the atom. This stirred a flurry of discussion about the interaction of radiation with electrons. Accounting for experimental data is the only way theoretical physicists have of testing the validity of their theories. Explaining the new data required modification of the 1928 Dirac equation which had been the cornerstone of quantum electrodynamics describing the behavior of electrons in atoms.

Hans Bethe was so intrigued by the new data that he spent the whole train ride back from New York City deriving a similar quantity from quantum perturbation theory. Although he encountered some difficulties and ignored the effects of relativity, he figured that he could work out the details later. He called Feynman from Schenectady, tremendously excited about his solution. Feynman didn't immediately understand how this was important. Only when Bethe mentioned in a lecture a few months later after he returned to Cornell that a relativistically (relating to the theory of relativity) invariant calculation was needed did Feynman perk up.

Feynman realized that the path integral methods and the ways of thinking about problems that he had used for his Ph.D. thesis avoided the difficulties in the standard quantum perturbation theory that Bethe had used. They also automatically took into account the changes in classical physics that occur near the speed of light. In other words, they were relativistically invariant. He went up to Bethe after the talk and said "I can do that for you. I'll bring it in for you tomorrow." It took a bit longer because in his haste Feynman made a mistake that he didn't straighten out until autumn 1947.

Feynman had mostly been tinkering with his method, using it as a visualizing tool. It had not previously occurred to him that he could calculate observable values that could be confirmed by experiment. Now he began using his path integrals to calculate all sorts of interesting physical properties. The more problems he tried, the more he learned the method would handle. He devised a shorthand, drawing diagrams that summarized complex mathematics, so that he could do the calculations faster. Soon he had an impressive toolkit for solving all sorts of problems in quantum electrodynamics.

Feynman was having a great deal of fun with his new equations, but he soon realized that he would have to publish his ideas if other people were to understand them. Writing up his work remained an onerous task for Feynman his whole career. Once he had finished a puzzle, he wanted to work on the next idea rather than enduring the drudgery of publication. He accepted the invitation of a colleague, Herbert Corben at the Carnegie Institute of Technology, and his wife to stay with them and write the paper. For a few days, Feynman avoided working on his paper: he played with the couple's children, went to the local fair, and told stories. As Corben recounted, "Finally he retired to his room and started to write. He was told by my wife [Mulaika] that he could not come out again until he had at least a rough draft." His paper was published in *Reviews of Modern Physics* in 1948.

Feynman had revamped quantum electrodynamics (QED), a theory that governs all interactions between electrons and radiation (light) and thus all chemical processes. Everything that happens outside of the nucleus of the atom is governed by QED and gravity. Feynman used his path-integral formulation to resolve the wave-particle duality of light. He could explain wave-like diffraction patterns and also particle-like photons that could be counted. In effect, he brought everyday classical mechanics in line with the built-in uncertainties in quantum mechanics.

A new graduate student arrived from England in September 1947, to work with Hans Bethe. Freeman Dyson was an English mathematical prodigy who soon recognized that not only was Feynman the liveliest person in the physics department, but he had come up with a method that could not only solve all of the problems the old quantum mechanics methods could, but also could solve many that the old methods could not. Dyson decided that he wanted to first understand Feynman's ideas and then to explain them in a way that other physicists could understand.

The Pocono Manor Conference, the second of the small conferences on the foundations of quantum physics, was held in the mountains of eastern Pennsylvania in April 1948. Dyson, still a student, was not invited. Julian Schwinger, only three months older than Feynman, was speaking at the conference. Schwinger's mathematically eloquent but convoluted and nearly unintelligible formulas (even to physicists) were laying a mathematical foundation for QED. Feynman was eager to show the distinguished audience how his intuitive methods gave the same results as Schwinger's complex mathematics. He believed that his treatment put a physical face on the mathematical derivation.

Schwinger gave a polished presentation on his latest formulation of quantum electrodynamics. Feynman's talk, "An Alternative Formulation of Quantum Electrodynamics" was a disaster. Bethe had suggested to him that more people at the meeting would appreciate a mathematical approach. Using mathematics to explain his new system rather than the physical intuition that he used to derive it was a tactical error.

Freeman Dyson had a distinguished career as a physicist and engineer.

When he tried to recover by switching to his intuitive explanation, Feynman ended up totally confusing his audience.

Feynman was tormented by his failure to get his ideas across in this forum of the world's most distinguished physicists. Later on he said, "I had too much stuff. My machines came from too far away." Schwinger and Feynman later discussed their ideas over lunch and concluded that their different world views gave the same answer.

In June, the school year ended, and Feynman prepared to set off in his secondhand Oldsmobile to look for adventure. Dyson was scheduled after a two-week break to attend a summer course on QED given by Julian Schwinger at the University of Michigan in Ann Arbor, but before leaving, Feynman invited Dyson to accompany him on a cross country drive to New Mexico. Dyson jumped at the chance.

One night holed up in a cheap hotel in Oklahoma and kept awake by the pouring rain, Dyson and Feynman talked through the night. Dyson listened as Feynman told about Arline, his work on the bomb, and of course, physics. Dyson realized why Feynman was having a hard time convincing others of his ideas.

"Nobody but Dick could use his theory, because he was always invoking his intuition to make up the rules of the game as he went along. Until the rules were codified and made mathematically precise, I could not call it a theory." In Albuquerque they parted and Dyson caught a Greyhound bus back east for Ann Arbor and his summer course.

Later that summer, Dyson was struck by an understanding of how Feynman and Schwinger's approaches could be integrated. He also took into account the work of Sin-Itiro Tomonaga, a Japanese physicist who studied QED independently. Dyson wrote a paper, "The Radiation Theories of Tomonaga, Schwinger, and Feynman," for *Physical Review*, focusing on harmonizing the different approaches. This piece of work made QED accessible to the average physicist, established Dyson's reputation, and converted Feynman's diagrams into a standardized set of graphs.

After some initial resistance, the Feynman-Dyson graphs or Feynman diagrams became accepted tools in the trade. At the American Physical Society meeting in January 1949, Dyson and Feynman sat together while speaker after speaker acknowledged the Feynman-Dyson theory. Feynman turned to Dyson and said, "Well, Doc, you're in." In April 1949, at the third and final conference on the foundation of quantum physics, the topic was Feynman's approach to QED. A month shy of his thirty-first birthday, Richard Feynman was confirmed as the foremost physicist in his generation.

Over the following three years Feynman published a series of six papers that laid the foundation for the next generation of quantum physics. They explained his space-time representation of quantum interactions at work in solving a variety of problems. He insisted on the plainest statements about energy, time, and space, and wrote in the simplest terms. The Feynman diagrams became the standard way to do QED calculations. Most importantly, the results agreed well with experimental data.

In spite of the acceptance of his ideas by the physics community, Feynman remained restless. He was still living on campus and his social life was still chaotic. The stream of job offers since Los Alamos had not lessened, and he began to look at them more seriously. With his newfound rise to prominence he was feeling stifled. At Cornell, Hans Bethe would always be the star; Feynman had higher ambitions.

He wrote Robert Bacher, a Los Alamos acquaintance who was trying to build a modern physics department at Caltech in Pasadena, California. Caltech was a technology institute focusing on science and engineering. It sounded like a place where Feynman would feel at home.

While Bacher began the arrangements to bring Feynman to Caltech, Feynman grew frustrated by the winter weather in Ithaca. One day while kneeling in the slush, attaching tire chains with numbed fingers so he could get up slippery brick-paved Buffalo Street, he decided that he had to find a place with a warmer climate. An invitation to spend six weeks teaching at the new Centro Brasileiro de Pesquisas Físicas (Brazilian Center for Physics Research) in Rio de Janeiro during the summer of 1949 sounded good. He quickly arranged a cram course with a graduate student in Portuguese (the language of Brazil) and traveled to the South American country. With some difficulty he gave his series of lectures in Portuguese. While there, he greatly enjoyed the relaxed lifestyle, the sunny beaches, and the nightlife.

Back in Ithaca at the end of January 1950, he took a month leave from Cornell to give a series of lectures on quantum dynamics and meson theories at Caltech. Shortly after he returned from California, Caltech offered Feynman a professorship of theoretical physics. It was the snows of Ithaca against the palm trees of Southern California. Feynman made his decision. After giving a series of talks in Paris and Geneva on his first trip to Europe in April 1950, he was ready to move on.

Richard Feynman stands before a blackboard in his class-room, 1950s. Teaching duties did not prevent Feynman from pursuing what he believed was his most important work—research. Feynman enjoyed wrestling with difficult physics problems, which he considered puzzles to be solved.

CHAPTER FIVE

"There Was a Moment When I Knew How Nature Works"

B efore beginning at Caltech, Feynman spent the summer of 1950 as a consultant at the Institute for Numerical Analysis at UCLA. Feynman ran into Mark Kac, a Polish mathematician from Cornell who was also at UCLA for the summer and they worked on some problems together. Kac had been using a method similar to Feynman's path integral and had published a formula in 1949, later called the Feynman-Kac Formula, which had become a much used mathematical tool linking probability and quantum mechanics.

As part of his recruitment, Caltech had offered him a sabbatical year from 1951-1952. He was drawn back to the beaches and nightlife of Rio de Janeiro and the Center for Physics Research. The U.S. State Department Point Four Program and Caltech covered his salary for the ten-month stay in Brazil, and Feynman returned to the South American country in August 1951.

Feynman greatly enjoyed life in Brazil. He was intrigued by the inviting beat of the street music in Copacabana which appealed to him as a drummer. He taught himself to play the *frigideira*, a small tin pan with a beater, and joined a local samba group. They performed at private parties and took part in the famous Rio Carnaval festival.

Feynman lived at the Miramar Palace Hotel in Copacabana and often would go to a bar late in the evening for a few drinks with the stewardesses and pilots from Pan Am Airlines who stayed at the hotel during their stopovers in Rio. The next morning he would be back at the university to give his lectures.

One afternoon after finishing his lecture for the day, Feynman was walking past a bar across from the beach and felt an overpowering craving for a cocktail. Then he realized that he was alone, it was the middle of the afternoon, and there was no social reason to drink. The feeling of being out of control was strong enough to scare him, and he never drank alcohol after that. "I get so much fun out of thinking that I don't want to destroy this most pleasant machine that makes life such a great kick." The experience didn't keep him out of bars, however. He found the people much too interesting.

Even though he appreciated the relaxed South American atmosphere and spent many afternoons on the beach, Feynman was not one to rest quietly. With J. Leite Lopes, the co-founder of the Center for Physics Research, he set out to apply his new quantum electrodynamics tools to understand the nuclear structure of the deuteron, an isotope of the simplest atom, hydrogen. The deuteron was complicated because it contained a neutron made up of smaller particles called mesons, in addition to the proton in its nucleus. Feynman and Lopes modified the theory which accurately described hydrogen to account for the mesons in the deuteron, creating the pseudoscalar meson theory.

Feynman taught graduate students at the Center. In the mornings at the University of Rio de Janeiro, he taught mathematical methods and an electricity and magnetism course. Although the students were interested and diligently took notes, unlike his students at Cornell, the Brazilian students

Brazilian theoretical physicist Jose Leite Lopes (1918–2006) had studied under Albert Einstein at Princeton before co-founding the Brazilian Center for Physics Research (Centro Brasileiro de Pesquisas Físicas).

never asked questions no matter how far he strayed from their textbook. They also never turned in any of the problems that he gave them to solve. That disturbed him because for him doing problems was the way to really learn physics.

Feynman soon discovered that the students couldn't do the problems because they were memorizing definitions instead of understanding the science and developing a feel for problem solving. Feynman worked against this, believing it wasn't enough for students to just know the basic definitions of physics concepts, but that they be able to practically apply them as well.

Despite Feynman's busy schedule in Brazil, there remained an emptiness. He was fast approaching what would have been his and Arline's tenth wedding anniversary in 1952, and he was lonely. While showing an airline flight attendant around the Egyptian display in the Rio museum on a date and telling her about the art on a sarcophagus, he was reminded that he had learned about art from Mary Louise Bell, an art history major he knew from Cornell now living in Westwood, near Pasadena.

They had dated, but the relationship had been stormy. Impulsively, Feynman wrote her a letter proposing marriage. He reminisced later, "Someone who's wise could have told me that [proposing] was dangerous: When you're away and you've got nothing but paper, and you're feeling lonely, you remember all the good things and you can't remember the reasons you had the arguments."

Feynman and Mary Louise Bell were married in June of 1952, after he returned from Brazil. Their relationship continued to be tense: Bell wanted to be married to a professor who observed proper decorum in dress and behavior, and thought physicists were bores and refused to socialize with them. She and Feynman divorced in the summer of 1956. Feynman agreed to admit to extreme cruelty, and Bell testified that his bongo drumming made a terrible noise and that he did calculus in bed.

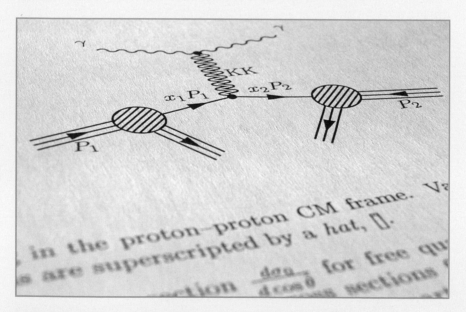

Feynman's method of illustrating the movement of subatomic particles became known as Feynman diagrams.

Feynman began his career at Caltech in 1952. He collected physics puzzles that interested him. Whenever he was satisfied with one problem or was frustrated at not finding a suitable answer, he would set it aside and begin work on another problem. Because of this, some people considered Feynman to be a dilettante, never finishing off a piece of work before moving on to a new area. He didn't care what they thought, though. Feynman's satisfaction was in figuring out the puzzle. When the puzzle was solved, the problem was of no more interest, unless it generated another puzzle. And whenever someone entered a new area of physics they would find that "Feynman had signed the guestbook and already left."

He had developed his own tool kit of methods replete with shortcuts and cultivated his ability, unfathomable to others, to break down any situation in physics to its simplest components and to visualize the interactions. Feynman didn't care if the Greeks had solved a problem thousands of years ago or if a solution had been published last week in *Physical Review*. His interest was solving the problem himself, and almost always by a completely different route. Unlike other physicists, he rarely read the physics literature and declined to review papers submitted to journals. He feared he might read something that would spoil his game.

One of the puzzles Feynman had contemplated back at Cornell, but had put away while he was finishing up his study of quantum electrodynamics, was the problem of the superfluidity of liquid helium. Helium is a gas under normal conditions of temperature and pressure. In 1908, Heike Onnes in Holland had managed to condense helium into a liquid at only 5.2 degrees Kelvin above absolute zero, the temperature at which all molecular motion was expected to stop. But in helium at 2.2 degrees above absolute zero and below, the liquid helium would flow spontaneously through narrow tubes with no resistance. It would crawl up the side of a vessel through a tube into a vessel kept at a higher temperature. The liquid would also pass through holes too small to allow helium gas through. This cold helium was a superfluid. Once a superfluid was started in motion, it would continue to move indefinitely, suffering no friction or viscosity.

The main hypotheses to explain these properties were that either the transition at 2.2 degrees Kelvin was a general quantum property of liquids or that it was strictly due to the quantum behavior of the helium atoms themselves. A key observation that would provide a clue was that this transition was seen only with the He^4 isotope and not with the He^3 isotope. The different numbers of neutrons in the nuclei (two and one, respectively), are a difference that effects the quantum mechanical states of the atoms. Feynman theorized that the phenomenon had to do with the quantum states of the He^4 atoms.

The He^4 quantum states obey a set of conditions called Bose statistics that normally govern subatomic particles like photons, which are often thought of as waves. Electrons and He^3 atoms, on the other hand, obey different conditions called Fermi statistics which are for particles that have a property called quantum spin. The Bose and Fermi statistics govern the energy level structure of the atoms they describe and thus how they respond to the amount of energy available (temperature).

Feynman used his path integral methods, adapting them to He^4, which obeyed Bose statistics, and found that they produced results that fit the experimental data quite well. Quantum theory, unlike classical theory, predicts that molecular motion does not completely stop at absolute zero temperature. That would violate the Heisenberg uncertainty principle which is the basis for the success of all quantum theories. The principle forbids exact knowledge of position and energy of any object. This difference is too small to be noticeable for everyday things but is important for things the size of atoms. At

Cryogenic containers used for storing liquid helium in a warehouse at Cornell University. Helium exists naturally as a gas, but will become liquid under high pressure and at extremely low temperatures (-450° Fahrenheit / -267° Celsius).

absolute zero there is enough motion of the collection of He^4 molecules to satisfy this tiny energy difference.

Feynman wanted to arrive at a solution using pure visualization. He tried to imagine what the infinitesimal motions would look like that could account for the smallest energy level changes he calculated. He visualized tiny vortices, like miniature smoke rings one atom in diameter stacked to form strings, and he called them rotons. His path integrals could deal with this, and a new set of Feynman diagrams was created.

In his longest series of papers on one topic—ten, published from 1953–1958—Feynman and one of his few graduate students, Michael Cohen, refined his concepts on superfluidity and struggled with explaining its corollary, superconductivity. Superconductivity occurs in some substances when they are cooled to very close to absolute zero. A superconducting wire will pass electrical current without any resistance much like superfluids move without friction. A superconducting electromagnet could be started with a single pulse of current which would continue circulating in the magnet windings generating a magnetic field, theoretically forever.

Feynman's interest in superconductivity began with an article by British physicist Herbert Fröhlich on the movement of electrons in a salt crystal. The interaction of the electrons with quantum mechanical states of the crystal lattice created subatomic particles called polarons which governed properties similar to conductivity. He recognized that he could apply his path integral approach to polarons in a crystal, and derived a new set of Feynman diagrams. They were helpful for solid-state physicists, but for Feynman, polarons were a side issue. He published a single paper in 1955 on slow electrons in crystals, but spent a great deal of time and many pages of calculations trying to extend the polaron theory to superconductivity.

In 1956, Feynman admitted defeat on superconductivity. He gave a talk at a conference where he explained what he had tried in excruciating detail and how he had failed. In the end he mused that he simply didn't have enough imagination. Such admissions are rarely heard in science where only the successes are published.

In 1957, a successful superconductivity theory was pro-duced by John Bardeen and colleagues Leon Cooper and Robert Schrieffer. Feynman was one of the first to realize that the Bardeen team had found the solution and support-ed its adoption.

As Feynman hit his mid-thirties during the 1950s, his contri-butions to the world of physics began receiving recognition. Feynman maintained a love-hate relationship with those who would accord him honors. He very much craved acceptance, but at the same time he despised empty honors. Honorary degrees particularly irked him. He had worked hard for his Ph.D., which he believed stood for a certain degree of compe-tence. The idea of an unearned degree was unacceptable.

In January 1954, Feynman picked up the phone to find Lewis Strauss, chairman of the Board of Trustees of the Institute for Advanced Study at Princeton and chairman of the Atomic Energy Commission, on the line. Thinking that Strauss was going to ask him to do something for the Commission,

Feynman was stunned to hear that he had been awarded the Albert Einstein Prize, one of the highest honors in American science. Established by Strauss and his wife in 1949, the award consisted of a gold medal, $15,000, and a citation.

"Won? Hot Dog!" Feynman responded to the news. He didn't believe in awards as an honor, but this one paid good money. He did have one problem with accepting the award. He would have to go to Washington in March to receive it from Strauss, whom he disliked personally. Lewis Strauss had played a key role in the 1953 government hearings denying Robert Oppenheimer security clearance for secret U.S. Government work. Besides respecting his former boss as a physicist, Feynman had never forgotten that Oppenheimer had made arrangements at the sanatorium in Albuquerque for Arline when Feynman joined Los Alamos. Feynman had testified at the 1953 hearings in favor of Oppenheimer.

At first Feynman plotted to embarrass Strauss by refusing the award at the ceremony, but he was convinced not to do this by Isidor Rabi, a respected physicist visiting Caltech. Rabi advised, "A man's generosity should never be used as a weapon against him." Feynman accepted the award; the money went for a down payment on a beach house at La Mision, Baja California.

In the fall of 1955, Robert Hellwarth joined the Caltech physics department as a research assistant from Oxford, England, and gave a seminar on a new kind of quantum mechanical amplifier, dubbed the maser (molecular amplification by stimulated emission), that had been his Ph.D. thesis project. Feynman immediately became interested in the possibility of studying the interactions among quantum states. Feynman, Hellwarth, and Frank Vernon, an engineer from the Aerospace Corporation, spent months in front of a blackboard discussing the theory behind the phenomenon.

In a maser, microwave energy of a particular frequency is focused on a vacuum chamber containing a small amount of

Feynman in his office at Caltech, 1959.

ammonia gas. The ammonia absorbs the microwaves and emits an amplified microwave signal of an extremely pure and stable frequency. Masers were potentially useful as amplifiers and as exquisitely sensitive detectors, but the engineers trying to design devices were stymied by the laborious calculations required in the years before computers.

Feynman, Hellwarth, and Vernon developed a system of simple diagrams based on Feynman's path integral formulation that provided answers of equal or greater accuracy than the pages of calculations. The visual display was simple for students and practical for working engineers.

Still, the paper resulting from Feynman's collaboration with Hellwarth and Vernon initially did not generate much interest. Disappointed, Feynman commented, "Townes and others who knew quantum mechanics were also doing it. If I had never existed, nobody would have noticed the difference." Feynman later said, "It was quite powerful. But it wasn't much used by people. They derived the same results by more conventional methods with which they felt more comfortable." However, by 1958 the optical version of the maser, the laser, had been described. The new device required the same kind of calculations Feynman had worked on, and their paper became one of Feynman's most cited publications.

Hellwarth moved on to Hughes Aircraft Company in nearby Culver City, California, in 1956 and invited Feynman to give a series of lectures to the scientists and engineers at Hughes on mutually interesting topics. Feynman clearly enjoyed the contact with applied science. He continued giving his weekly two-hour lecture every Wednesday into the 1980s.

Despite his output, Feynman was dissatisfied. He believed he was only solving little questions that amused him, but was failing to reach beyond nature's surface to uncover fundamental principles. The stubborn superconductivity problem had consumed much of his energy. It prevented him from working on deeper questions of how the universe worked, and frustrated him. He was approaching another crisis of confidence.

During the late 1950s and early 1960s, new subatomic particles were being regularly discovered using the atomic particle accelerators coming on line. The accelerators smashed protons and electrons into atoms and into each other at ever increasing energies. Most of an atom is empty space, but at the core resides the tiny densely packed nucleus. If the energy of the projectile is right, the energy of the collision is converted into other kinds of particles. Many of the new entities were unstable and would rapidly decay into other particles.

Physicists divide forces of nature into four types: gravitational, electromagnetic, a strong force holding the nucleus together, and the so-called weak force involved in radioactive decay and certain other particle decays. Quantum electrodynamics, particularly Feynman's contributions, had dealt with the electromagnetic force satisfactorily. However, the same approach did not work well for the other forces.

For electrodynamics the simplest Feynman diagrams dominated the solution, but a large number of terms and thus many diagrams were required to describe the other forces. In order to understand the new particles being created in the accelerators, physicists postulated a host of abstract symmetries, conservation laws, and quantum numbers. These were unsatisfactory because they were ad hoc, created after the observations, not predicted by theory derived from first principles.

The weak force, which is weak only by comparison to the strong nuclear force, governs a type of radioactive decay called β-decay (beta decay). The decay is the spontaneous disintegration of a neutron into a proton, an electron, and a massless, chargeless particle called a neutrino. This reaction and its governing weak force were presumed to obey certain conservation laws because the other forces, the electromagnetic force and the strong force, obeyed similar conservation laws.

In 1956, there was a controversy over one of these rules: the conservation of a property called parity. Two new particles, theta and tau, were distinguished because theta decayed into two pion particles while tau decayed into three pions. Theta and tau were identical in other properties such as their mass. According to the conversation of parity property, theta and tau must be different particles. At the 1956 Rochester Conference on High Energy Nuclear Physics, Feynman asked, "Could it be that theta and tau are different parity states of the same particle which has no definite parity, i.e. that parity is not conserved? That is, does nature have a way of defining right- or left-handedness uniquely? What would happen if parity were wrong? What would be wrong with that in physics?"

Feynman's comment caused two young physicists, Chen Ning Yang and Tsung Dao Lee, to investigate the possibilities. Within a year they had evidence that nature really did distinguish left and right at its core, earning them a Nobel Prize. Their paper was to be presented at the 1957 Rochester Conference.

Feynman was staying with his sister Joan before the Conference. She had finished her Ph.D. in solid state physics at Syracuse and was living there now. He was feeling unproductive and complained to her that he wasn't able to work any more, that the ideas weren't coming. She quickly dismissed that excuse, saying that his real problem was that he never stayed with one idea long enough to finish it.

Feynman had been given the Yang and Lee paper, but couldn't understand it. Like he advised her when she was four-teen and couldn't understand the astronomy textbook, Joan said, "No, what you mean is not that you don't understand it. You didn't invent it. If you sat down like a graduate student and quietly went through the paper, line by line, you'd understand it." He went upstairs, and did as he was told.

Reading the paper jogged him into action. It wasn't long before he thought of an alternative formulation for parity. He went back to the very simplest model and re-derived equations for neutron decay using his path integral approach. It worked, except for some mismatches of his the-ory with the Yang and Lee predictions and some of the trans-formations among the particles, but he felt he could work out the details later. It was a major discovery. "There was a moment when I knew how nature worked. It had elegance and beauty," he recalled.

He knew that he had something special. Dirac had discov-ered the equation for the electron and the basis for quantum electrodynamics, and now from first principles, Feynman had discovered the equation for the neutrino and the basis for the weak interaction. "I felt that I knew something that no one else knew about [that] law of nature. This was nothing like the work of Maxwell or Dirac, but it was the only law of nature I could lay a claim to."

Instead of publishing, Feynman went for the summer back to Brazil and continued to puzzle over the discrepancies between his formation and the Yang and Lee predictions. When he got back to Caltech in the fall he was excited to hear that a colleague in the physics department, Murray Gell-Mann, had come to a similar conclusion about the kind of interactions among the particles. Gell-Mann was not pleased to find that someone else was on the same track, but after much discussion, argument, and a not-so-subtle recommendation from their department chairman, they decided to publish together.

Their joint paper, "Theory of the Fermi Interaction" was only six pages long. Their theory was broad in scope, extending beyond beta decay to other kinds of particle interactions. It made predictions that kept experimentalists busy for years. The paper signaled the start of a fruitful collaboration between two scientists who couldn't have been any more different temperamentally. They would continue to stimulate and needle each other the rest of Feynman's life.

CHAPTER SIX

Teacher

I n the spring of 1958, Richard Feynman attended an international conference on the peaceful uses of atomic energy at Lake Geneva. He was giving a summary of his and Murray Gell-Mann's weak interaction theory at the request of the U.S. State Department. The Russians had launched the world's first satellite, Sputnik, on October 4, 1957, and the American government wanted a public relations counter to the Russians at the meeting.

While relaxing at the Lake Geneva beach, a flash of blue caught Feynman's attention, one of the new two-piece bathing suits called a bikini. Gweneth Howarth, a twenty-four-year-old jeweler's daughter from Ripponden in Yorkshire, England, was wearing the suit. She noticed Feynman looking at her, and surprised him by saying in English that the lake water was very cold. She was working as an au pair in Switzerland, taking care of a family's children and saving her twenty-five dollar a month earnings. Feynman immediately offered her twenty dollars a week to be his housekeeper. She refused: she had her room and board paid and plenty of boyfriends.

Richard Feynman speaks to a class at Caltech, 1959. Feynman became known as the "Great Explainer" because of his belief that scientific principles should be taught at a level that a college freshman could understand. In 1972, the American Association of Physics Teachers recognized his contribution to teaching by awarding Feynman the Oersted Medal, the organization's highest honor.

Feynman convinced Gweneth to accompany him to a night-club where they talked for hours. She had found life in her Yorkshire town confining and had left to find some excitement and was saving her money for an around the world trip. Feynman was impressed with her daring, realizing that Gweneth was the first woman that he had met who shared his sense of high adventure and wanderlust. Before he left Geneva, Gweneth promised to consider his offer to work for him.

They continued to correspond, and finally Gweneth agreed to come to the United States. She filed the necessary papers at the U.S. Consulate in Zurich while Feynman got Matthew Sands, a friend of his, and Sands' wife to sign as third-party employers for Gweneth. After many months her visa finally came through and Feynman wrote her, "I was over-joyed to hear that you are coming at last! We have been wait-ing so long.! What did you finally do to the embassy to wake them up? I need you more than ever—I'm getting sick of my own meals."

Gweneth arrived in June 1959 and immediately took over his household. There was a lot to do. Since his divorce from Mary Lou Bell, Feynman had reduced his domestic side to a bare minimum. Bell had taken all of the household furni-ture in the divorce. He owned five identical pairs of shoes, five identical blue suits, white shirts, and no ties. It made life easier—no decisions on what to wear. Keys, wallet, and loose coins went in the same pockets every day so he wouldn't have to waste energy finding them. He refused to own a radio or a television.

From the beginning, Gweneth made it clear that she was to have her own life. Feynman lived in the front of the house, and she had her own room in the back. She soon had sever-al boyfriends, but also dated Feynman. Her presence was a secret at first to all except a few close friends, but soon the regulars at the dining hall in the Atheneum faculty club noticed that Feynman was going home for lunch. Then Gweneth and Feynman began appearing at parties together.

In the spring of 1960, Feynman realized that he was more content than he had been in years, and knew that Gweneth was the reason. He wanted to propose, but this time he was patient, having learned from his impulsive, disastrous marriage to Mary Lou Bell. He marked a date on his calendar. If he felt the same about her after a few weeks, he would propose. When the date arrived, he still wished to marry Gweneth, and took the next step.

His proposal caught her completely unaware, and she made him wait until the next day for an answer: yes. They were married on September 24, 1960, at the Pasadena Huntington Hotel. He was forty-two years old and she was twenty-six.

While his personal life stabilized, Feynman's interests remained varied. Topics such as DNA and the genetic code intrigued him, but were out of his intellectual realm. Feynman had a sabbatical year coming up in 1959-60. He decided that rather than going to another country to work on physics, he would stay at Caltech and work in a different field. He made arrangements with Max Delbrück, a physicist turned molecular biologist, to learn about molecular biology.

Scientists were only just beginning to understand the workings of life at the molecular level. The double helix structure of DNA had been described by James Watson and Francis Crick in the early 1950s, but the mechanism of how the genetic code was read or how changes in the code—mutations—had their effects was still unknown.

Feynman joined the lab of Matt Meselson in Delbrück's department to work on mechanisms of mutation. He had to learn how to handle an experimental system, the T4 virus, which infected the common bacterium *E. coli.* At first he found it difficult. Biology experiments were messier and did not reproduce as cleanly as physics experiments.

Gweneth and Richard Feynman dance at a formal affair, 1965.

He was studying a particular mutation, r₄₃, in the rII gene which would switch the ability of T4 to grow on one host strain of *E. coli* to another *E. coli* strain. Rare reverse mutations would convert a mutant T4 back into an apparently normal T4 that would grow on the original *E. coli* host strain. Feynman had noticed that some of the back mutated T4 looked different and called them idiot r's. He was able to show that these strange T4 were the result of a second mutation within the rII gene. His colleagues called them Feyntrons. Try as they might, neither Feynman nor Meselson had a complete explanation. This phenomenon was also noticed by other researchers at other institutions around the

same time and became known to biologists as intragenic suppression. In 1966, Watson and Crick used the concept of intragenic suppression to explain at a molecular level that mutations caused misspelling of the DNA "words" by removing or inserting pieces of DNA.

While working with Meselson, Feynman greatly enjoyed teaching first-year graduate biology students basic techniques, as well as probability and the statistics they needed to interpret their experiments. Many of the students didn't know that Feynman was a professor of physics. At the end of the year they rated him as the best teaching assistant. He said, "I got a tremendous boost by obtaining the best score of all teaching assistants; even in biology, not my field, I could explain things clearly, and I was rather proud of it."

With his sabbatical year learning about biology over, Feynman returned to the physics department, and was soon

Feynman's ability to explain complex issues in an easy-to-understand way, his humor, and his animated lecture style made him extremely popular among both Caltech students and colleagues.

drawn into a major project with his friend Matthew Sands. Sands was dissatisfied with the traditional nature of both the undergraduate and graduate physics curriculum at Caltech. He had known Feynman at Cornell and at Los Alamos and appreciated Feynman's ability to communicate complex ideas. "Anyone who had heard him lecture wanted to do so again. . . . His lectures had a light and airy feeling, to the extent that there were those who compared them to a Chinese meal, which one greatly enjoyed while one ate it with gusto, felt full with the feast of taste and flavor, but shortly after eating it felt hungry again." Sands enlisted Feynman's help in revising the graduate physics curriculum.

As a member of the Commission on College Physics, a national group established to improve physics teaching in the U.S., Sands felt that the physics being taught to undergraduates was stuck in the eighteenth and nineteenth centuries, and was outmoded. There was no mention until late in the second year of the course of the new understanding of the atom developed over the last twenty years in physics.

Robert Bacher, the department chairman, thought that Sands was too radical. With the support of some of the younger members of the physics department faculty, Sands managed to convince Bacher that the curriculum should be brought up to date. To rein in Sands, though, Bacher appointed Robert Leighton and another conservative faculty member to help revise the introductory physics course. At first they couldn't agree on a course outline. Finally, Sands suggested, "Look, why don't we get Feynman to give the lectures and let him make the final decision on the contents?"

He went to Feynman's house to propose the idea. Sands caught him at the right time. Feynman had not started a new major research problem, and he was still rethinking his goals after his rejuvenating sabbatical foray into biology. Sands knew that the best way to catch Feynman's interest was to offer him a challenge; he said, "Look, Richard, you have spent forty years trying to understand physics. Now here is your chance to distill it down to the essence at the level of a freshman." Feynman wasn't sure because he had not taught freshmen before, but he said would think about it. A few days later Feynman agreed to teach the course.

Feynman put all of his time and energy into the project, not only planning but choreographing each lecture, designing and coordinating new demonstrations and explanations. There was no textbook, only his lectures and recitation sections in which graduate students would provide further explanation of the concepts. Leighton, Sands, and Feynman met at lunch after each lecture to judge the student response and talk about the course. He gave two lectures a week, bringing with him a single slip of paper to remind himself of the points he wanted to make.

The lectures were recorded, with the intent to produce a textbook. This eventually was accomplished, but it was delayed by Feynman's unwillingness to spend his time writing. He would only edit what someone else wrote. Nearly all of his books were written this way. Feynman gives full credit to Sands and Leighton for translating his words and his intent into the three-volume *Feynman Lectures on Physics* (which is still sold in campus bookstores).

Although he tremendously enjoyed the experience and judged it worth the effort, Feynman also was left with some doubts. "At the end of two years [1961-63] I felt that I had wasted two years, that I had done no research during this entire period, and I was muttering to this effect. I remember Robert Walker saying to me: 'Some day you will realize what you did for physics in those two years is far more important than any research you could have done during the same period.'"

The consensus of the physics community was that the *Lectures* were a major advance in teaching physics. Although they did not work for everyone because Feynman's breezy style could disguise the profound insights that were being developed, the *Lectures* delivered a healthy shakeup to the teaching of university physics.

Despite his success as a teacher, Feynman never developed a "school" of doctoral students who trained with him and who would carry on his work. His colleagues suggest that this was because of his unique style, which could not be learned. Feynman put the failure on himself. "I've put a lot of energy into students, but I think I wreck them somehow. I have never had a student that I felt I did something for, and I have never had a student who hasn't disappointed me in some way. I don't think I did very well."

One reason was that he refused to be responsible for showing students how to be successful. He expected them to show initiative to come up with their own problems to work on. Because he was interested in so many things, it was hard for him not to jump in and solve a mystery. He would call himself a fool when he made a mistake, and was not shy about describing students or faculty members the same way. This critical attitude, while making him a successful physicist, made him hard to get close to, and did not increase a student's feeling of self worth. However, whenever a student had a physics question, Feynman would talk with him or her. Faculty members had to wait.

On December 29, 1959, Feynman gave a lecture at the American Physical Society annual meeting, held at Caltech that year. Miniaturization had become a popular concept in the world of electronics as vacuum tubes gave way to the transistor. Feynman's thinking was far ahead of many others on this topic. He wondered on what size scale would quantum mechanical effects be noticeable in the everyday (classical physics) world.

In his lecture "There's Plenty of Room at the Bottom" he talked about testing limits to how small things could be made. Starting with the human eye's resolution of about 1/120 of an inch, he calculated that a dot that size could be shrunk by a factor of 25,000 and still be represented by an image of a dot about thirty atoms across. The entire *Encyclopedia Britannica* could be printed on the head of a single pin without loss of resolution and read with an electron microscope.

In the early 1960s computers were room-sized. It was clear that they needed to be made smaller, but it wasn't obvious how that could be done, or by how much. The techniques that would make desktop or laptop computers possible were decades away, yet Feynman was already thinking about even smaller devices. He wondered what the laws of physics would do to systems at such a small scale. At the level of atoms, quantum mechanics rule—bringing in all sorts of new forces, new difficulties, and new possibilities. "I am inspired by the biological phenomena in which chemical forces are used in a repetitious fashion to produce all sorts of weird effects," he said.

He announced two $1,000 prizes he was offering, one to build an operating electrical motor no larger than 1/64 inch in any dimension, and the other to anyone who could take the information on a page of a book and reduce it 25,000 times in size so that it could be read by an electron microscope.

Feynman was inundated by people claiming to have made the miniature motor, but there were no winners. Finally, in November 1960, William McClellan, an engineer at a local electronics company, lugged a grocery carton into Feynman's office. McClellan pulled a microscope out of his box to view his creation: a motor, the size of a speck, weighing 250 micrograms, containing thirteen parts, and capable of developing one-millionth of a horsepower. McClellan had spent two and a half months of lunch hours winding 1/2000 inch diameter copper wire with a sharpened toothpick and turning miniscule metal parts on a watchmakers lathe. The motor ran smoothly. Although building the tiny motor had not required any new concepts, which was what Feynman had hoped for, he had to admit that it met the criteria for the award. He had neglected to make arrangements to fund the prizes, so he wrote McClellan a personal check.

Fortunately for Feynman's finances, the second part of his challenge was not answered until 1985 when Tom Newton, a graduate student at Stanford University, wrote the first page of *A Tale of Two Cities* on the head of a pin. By that time, manipulation of objects at the atomic level was commonplace in the microelectronics industry. A whole industry had been based on the precepts set forth by Feynman some thirty years earlier. The field of nanotechnology which developed from Feynman's original ideas that physics might be different on the nanoscale

In his groundbreaking book *Philosophiæ Naturalis Principia Mathematica* (Mathematical Principles of Natural Philosophy, 1687), the English physicist and mathematician Isaac Newton (1643–1727) described the laws of gravitation and motion. These laws formed the foundation of classical physics. During some of his lectures, Feynman explored the connections between Newton's laws and the newer field of quantum physics.

is now poised to move beyond electronics into industry, biology, and medicine.

Feynman did not entirely forsake thinking about new theories even when he was immersed in his undergraduate lectures. In 1957, he had begun trying to explain gravity from a quantum perspective.

He was always uncomfortable with a quantum theory of gravity because experiments could not be done to verify predictions. Gravity is the weakest of all the forces observed every day, but with extremely long range. It therefore is usually observed acting between large masses such as planets, stars, and galaxies. Gravity becomes stronger than the other physical forces (electrical, weak nuclear, strong nuclear) only at short separations between objects. To atomic physicists this means that features of quantum gravity will be observed at only at unachievable particle accelerator energies, or by making impossibly accurate measurements, better than one part in 10^{120}.

Nevertheless, Feynman worked hard to create his own visual image of the problem. On Mondays during the 1962-1963 school year while he was giving the freshman lectures, he also gave a series of twenty-seven graduate lectures on his thoughts about gravitation. Sixteen of these lectures were transcribed and became the "Feynman Lectures on Gravitation." Although he was never able to arrive at a satisfactory theory that would allow computation, Feynman is credited, along with others, with having brought quantum mechanics to gravity.

The success of his student lectures had whetted Feynman's drive to communicate his scientific ideas. He gave a series of seven lectures at Cornell's annual Messenger Lecture series in November 1964, choosing as his topic "The Character of Physical Law." This time he was communicating with the general public rather than only physicists. He covered gravity, how mathematics is related to physics, probability and uncertainty, and distinguishing past and future. The lectures were recorded and broadcast by the British Broadcasting Corporation (BBC) followed by publication of a book. His exuberance and cultivated Long Island twang earned him a homespun reputation with the public, a common man who explained great ideas. He defined the essence of the scientific method, and made clear his own guiding philosophy about science. A new law is first postulated and is then used to make predictions.

> [Then] we compare the result of the computation to nature, with experiment or experience, compare it directly with observation to see if it works. If it disagrees with experiment, it is wrong. In that simple statement is the key to science. It does not make any difference how beautiful your guess is. It does not make any difference how smart you are, who made the guess, or what his name is—if it disagrees with experiment it is wrong.

Feynman and his three-year-old son, Carl, watch for the comet Ikeya-Seki outside their Altadena, California, home on October 21, 1965. Earlier that day, Feynman had been notified that he had been won the Nobel Prize in Physics.

CHAPTER SEVEN

A Change in Perspective

Feynman's friends and colleagues wondered how his third marriage would fare. Gweneth was sixteen years his junior, English, and very much determined to chart her own way in the world. The union could have been another disaster, like his rushed marriage to Mary Lou.

Gweneth, however, proved to be just what Feynman needed. She made up for his social deficiencies and gradually brought some order to his life. She said, "I don't feel [I'm a] shadow; I'm perfectly happy—not being a servant to him—we get along very well. I know he's happy because he says it. . . . I do it for the family, and I like it—I like to feel comfortable. This is where my satisfaction lies and I don't have to feel important. I do things that [Richard] doesn't do, and I do them well."

As his relationship with Gweneth progressed and deepened, Feynman began to temper his disregard for other people's sensibilities. He maintained his rigorous approach to science and his unique sensibilities, but he became an easier person to be around. However, he still refused to serve on faculty committees, write grant proposals, publish more than the bare minimum of articles, or do any of the myriad of other tasks that clutter academic life.

His life soon became both more complicated and more fulfilling. In 1962, while he prepared his freshman Lectures on Physics, Gweneth gave birth to their son Carl. Then in the midst of his transition into high energy physics, he and Gweneth adopted a two-month-old daughter, Michelle, in December 1968. Feynman settled easily into family life and began to recreate the relationship he'd shared with his father. As sharp and critical as he could be with graduate students or fellow faculty, he was relaxed and patient with Carl and Michelle. He spent hours playing games with them, telling stories, or being goofy. Carl loved the stories, the more fanciful the better, but Michelle would catch him if he tried to make something up.

When Carl and Michelle were of school age, Feynman began taking an interest in the way that children were taught math and science. He was angered when he found that just like when he was in school, understanding was considered less important than learning what he called hollow definitions. He proposed a simple test to decide if terms were being taught rather than ideas. "Without using the new word you have just learned, try to rephrase what you have just learned in your own language."

It was clear to him that though students learned definitions of terms, they were unable to use the concepts. He also knew that few of the high-level concepts being taught such as sets and number bases were actually used by anyone but mathematicians. They weren't even used by physicists. He decided he had to do something about it.

On March 14, 1963, Feynman was appointed to serve on the California state Curriculum Commission, which selected the grade school mathematics textbooks. Unlike the other textbook evaluators, who enlisted the help of teachers and administrators in their appraisals, he was determined to read all of the books. However, he had seriously underestimated the extent of the project. Three hundred pounds of books arrived from the state repository. Feynman had to build seventeen feet of shelving in his basement study to hold them all. He also had to fend off the representatives of the textbook publishing companies who were trying to convince the state to use their books.

Feynman found that the books were unsatisfactory. Gweneth said that it was like living over a volcano, when Feynman would explode at intervals over the uselessness of the books and the lack of knowledge of the authors.

Feynman, who refused to attend administrative meetings at Caltech, spent hours at meetings discussing the evaluations. He even traveled to Los Angeles several times to present his recommendations to the government committees that would be making the decisions. Feynman was annoyed and thought of quitting when he found that the final selection process paid little attention to the evaluations. He held out for one more term because the next year they would be considering science books. After looking at several of them he found that they were even more hopeless than the math books and resigned from the Commission. He didn't want to be associated with a group that wasn't accomplishing anything.

As his career progressed, various honorary organizations began courting Feynman. However, he held a special distaste for honorary organizations that did nothing other than promote the privilege of being a member and selected people who hadn't earned their recognition. This didn't stop the offers, though.

In April 1954, on the heels of having accepted the Einstein award, he was elected to the prestigious U.S. National Academy of Sciences. Feynman had never paid attention to anything that the group had done, and he was not impressed with what little physics he had read in their *Proceedings*. His department chair, Robert Bacher, and Paul Epstein, another faculty member, told

him that it was a great honor and urged him to accept the
nomination. Besides, many of his friends had worked hard to
nominate him.

Feynman decided to give the organization a chance and
went to Washington, D.C., to attend a meeting. He was appalled
by the lack of rigor of some of the biomedical presentations. He
wrote to the Academy president, Detlev W. Bronk, with his res-
ignation. "My desire to resign is merely a personal one; it is not
meant as a protest of any kind. . . . My peculiarity is this: I find it
psychologically very distasteful to judge other people's 'merit.'
. . . Maybe I don't explain it very well, but suffice it to say, I am
not happy as a member of a self-perpetuating honor society."
The Academy was reluctant to lose such a highly visible member
and kept asking what it could change for him to remain a member. He resigned in 1969, and finally in 1970 the Academy
relented and removed Feynman from its roster.

On October 21, 1965, Feynman was awakened at four in the
morning by the phone ringing. It was a correspondent from
the American Broadcasting Corporation:

> "Professor Feynman?"
>   "Hey! Why are you bothering me at this time in the
> morning?"
>   "I thought that you'd like to know that you've won
> the Nobel Prize."
>   "Yeah, but I'm sleeping! It would have been better if
> you had called me in the morning."

Feynman hung up, but the phone rang again and again.
Gweneth thought he was kidding her when he told her that he
had won the Nobel Prize for his work with electromagnetism
and dynamics. He went to his study and took the phone off the
hook so he could think about what he was going to do. Finally,
he put the phone back on the hook. It rang immediately. He
asked the caller, a correspondent from *Time* magazine, off the
record, if was there some way he could avoid accepting the

The California Institute of Technology (Caltech), where Feynman taught from 1952 to 1988, is a private research university located in Pasadena. The school's science and engineering programs are among the finest in the world. In addition to Richard Feynman, thirty other Caltech graduates or professors have won a Nobel Prize—the best ratio for any American university.

prize. They talked for a quarter of an hour and concluded that refusing would cause a bigger fuss than if he accepted the award. It was a sobering decision for Feynman. He was well aware that the Nobel Prize often marked the end of a scientific career and a signal that a scientist's years of creativity were over.

Reporters from the *Los Angeles Times* and the *Star-News* arrived by five that morning. Gweneth made coffee and Feynman did his best to answer their questions. Most wanted to know what he won the prize for, and they only wanted a simplified, easily understandable answer. He settled for saying that his contribution was devising a method to eliminate mathematical infinities which prevented solving calculations. He couldn't resist adding, only partly tongue in cheek, "We have designed a method for sweeping them under the rug." He posed for pictures with sleepy, three-year old Carl.

After the interviews were over a *Time* magazine reporter suggested that when asked for a one sentence explanation of what he did to deserve the Nobel Prize, Feynman's response should be, "Listen, buddy, if I could tell you in a minute what I did, it wouldn't be worth the Nobel Prize." Feynman wished he'd thought of it.

At nine that morning, the official telegram arrived, informing Feynman that he'd won the prize along with Julian Schwinger and Sin-Itiro Tomonaga for their work (done independently) with quantum electrodynamics.

Feynman shared the 1965 Nobel Prize in Physics with Japanese physicist Sin-Itiro Tomonaga (left, 1906-1979), and Julian Schwinger (top, 1918-1994). The three scientists had independently developed the theory of quantum electrodynamics (QED).

A news conference was held at the Atheneum at Caltech and the students hung a banner from the top of the Caltech administration building proclaiming "WIN BIG RPF." All day the phone rang with people offering their congratulations. The Feynmans didn't get to bed until after midnight.

A blizzard of letters and postcards began arriving from well-wishers all over the world. The ones Feynman appreciated the most were from friends, teachers, and schoolmates from Far Rockaway, MIT, and Princeton. He was pleased and surprised at how many people remembered him. Congratulations from colleagues also arrived, including a note with a suggestion from Isidor Rabi who had convinced him to accept the Einstein Award. "One word of advice from one whose great day was twenty-one years ago. Don't let it get you down. You will be even more on the shopping list of those who want to waste your time. Tell them to go to hell."

In the weeks leading up to the award ceremony in Stockholm, Sweden, on December 11, 1965, Feynman agonized over a particular requirement of the winning the Nobel: prize winners were expected to give two talks, an acceptance speech, and a longer, more technical lecture on their prize-winning work. It was the ten-minute acceptance address that caused Feynman the most anguish. He knew the science, so the technical talk would be easy, but the usual Thank-You speech would be hard to balance with the fact that he didn't want the award. How could he satisfy protocol and still be true to himself? Feynman proceeded to break with tradition for both talks.

In his acceptance speech he told the audience that he felt that he had already been given his prize in the satisfaction he gained from having made his discoveries and from the use that others were able to make of them. The biggest thrill he experienced as a result of the Prize arrived in the form of hundreds of letters from well-wishers after the announcement of the Nobel award.

For his Nobel address, Feynman chose to emphasize the path to discovery rather than the discoveries that lead to quantum electrodynamics. He reasoned that his co-prize winners Julian Schwinger and Sin-Itiro Tomonaga would cover the discoveries well enough. Instead of giving a polished view of the finished product, he wanted to portray the working reality of science. He described the sequence of ideas and circumstances, blind alleys, failures, and revelations that culminated in his discovery.

Feynman also managed to have some fun during the festivities, and Gweneth delighted in the experience. Her happiness was enough to override his doubts about whether he could go through with the whole thing. At a deeply personal level receiving the Nobel award did please him. Years later when he was asked which one person from the past he would want to bring back and talk to, Feynman replied "I'd like to bring back my father, so I could tell him I won the Nobel Prize."

The Feynmans return from Sweden to the U.S. was via Switzerland, where they stopped for Feynman to give a talk at CERN, the European particle physics facility. Still touchy about all of the honors heaped on him in Sweden, he wanted to let people know that he was the same old Feynman. He appeared on the podium dressed in the specially tailored suit he had worn to meet the King of Sweden and began his lecture saying that he had decided that he liked wearing a suit when he was giving a talk. The audience of physicists responded with jeers and catcalls until he stripped off the jacket and tie and continued his lecture in his customary shirtsleeves. He liked to say that CERN had straightened him out after hobnobbing with royalty.

The reality of the award and the changes that it would make in his life began to sink in. Everyone was going to take him seriously from now on. He didn't want—and would not accept—the responsibility. As he had decided after the war, he would be pointedly irresponsible. At lunch during his CERN visit, Victor Weisskopf, the director-general of the facility, and Feynman

Feynman accepts the 1965 Nobel Prize in Physics from King Gustaf VI of Sweden at a December 1965 ceremony.

made the following wager: "Mr. Feynman will pay the sum of Ten Dollars to Mr. Weisskopf if at any time during the next ten years (i.e. before 31 December 1975) the said Mr. Feynman has held a responsible position." Feynman collected on the bet in early 1976.

The Feynmans returned to home to a mountain of letters and postcards. Rabi had been correct about how much Fcynman would be in demand. He learned to be selective about responding to requests for a visit. The only invitations that he would accept other than to go to Japan or Brazil which he found exotic, were to visit science students in elementary, junior, or high schools, and then only if no teachers or school authorities attended and they didn't make a big deal over his

Feynman discusses quantum electrodynamics before an audience of European scientists at CERN, the world's largest particle physics laboratory, in 1965.

visit. Sometimes he would lecture at nearby universities in southern California, but he insisted on a low-key visit.

In January 1967, Feynman was delighted to refuse the offer of an honorary degree, from the University of Chicago. In his reply to the university president, George W. Beadle, after thanking him for the honor, he wrote: "However, I remember the work I did to get a real degree at Princeton and the guys on the same platform receiving honorary degrees without work. . . . It is like giving an 'honorary electricians license.' I swore then that if by chance I was offered one I would not accept it. Now at last (twenty-five years later) you have given me a chance to carry out my vow." He steadfastly refused every other offer of an honorary degree.

Feynman again began feeling the pressure of a lull in his scientific productivity. His focus on family after marrying Gweneth and the arrival of son Carl occupied his leisure moments, and he had put his physics on hold to devote his entire effort to revamping the freshman physics course. Then came the Nobel Prize with its continuing distractions. He was determined that he would not fall victim to the Prize. He reclaimed time and energy to work on physics again.

Feynman had encountered lapses in productivity before, but this time he was frightened because he feared being left behind by the rapid advances in modern physics. His salvation came from an unexpected source. In early 1967, he accepted an invitation to speak to the undergraduates at the University of Chicago. At breakfast in the Faculty Club there, he recognized James Watson, the co-discoverer with Francis Crick of the structure of DNA. They had become acquainted while Feynman was on sabbatical in the Caltech biology department. After they ate, Watson gave Feynman a manuscript for a memoir he called *Honest Jim* and asked for his opinion

After reading an unpublished manuscript by Dr. James D. Watson, an American scientist who had helped to uncover the molecular structure of DNA, Richard Feynman turned the focus of his own research in a new direction.

about the book. Watson's story of the discovery of the structure of the genetic material would later be published as *The Double Helix*.

Feynman read the book that evening, skipping a cocktail party being given at the faculty club in his honor. The outspokenness of the book resonated with Feynman's view of how science was done. He knew that it would provoke controversy. Later he wrote to Watson to give him his reaction. "Don't let anybody criticize that book who hasn't read it through to the end. . . . When you describe what went on in your head as the truth haltingly staggers upon you and passes on, finally fully recognized, you are describing how science is done. I know, for I have had the same beautiful and frightening experience."

When his meeting roommate David Goodstein, a Caltech physics Ph.D. student just finishing his degree, came up to go to bed, Feynman handed him the typescript and told him he had to read it. Feynman paced around and doodled on a pad until Goodstein finished the book near dawn. Goodstein's comment was "You know, it's amazing that Watson made this great discovery even though he was so far out of touch with what everyone in his field was doing." Feynman held up the pad on which the capital letters DISREGARD were written. He said, "That's what I've forgotten." He needed to start fresh.

CHAPTER EIGHT

Nuclear Structure

Feynman's revelation from reading Watson's book to disregard what other people were doing set him free. His self-imposed pressure was off and all of physics lay before him. So far during his career he had made ground-breaking discoveries for three of the four recognized forces of nature: electromagnetism (for which he had received the Nobel Prize), quantum gravity, and the weak nuclear force. A physicist normally worked in only one area of physics, and rarely contributed anything significant after the age of fifty. Now at age fifty-two, Feynman was determined not to succumb to the jinx of the Nobel Prize. There were still too many interesting problems he wanted to tackle. Feynman readied his toolbox of mathematical tricks to tackle the one remaining unexplained force of nature, the strong nuclear force.

An atom is mostly empty space with the electron orbits thinly spread over some distance from the tiny dense nuclear core containing protons and neutrons. The strong nuclear force was theorized to squeeze the protons and neutrons in the nucleus together against the electromagnetic repulsion between the like-charged protons. It was a hot topic that engaged physicists all over the world. The conceptual framework Feynman had built to understand the weak nuclear force and how β-radioactive decay occurred gave him a starting point. He wanted to explain how new particles were formed when electrons or protons, accelerated to near the speed of light, crashed into the nuclei of normal matter, such as a piece of metal foil, or into another high-speed beam of particles.

A constellation of new forms of matter appeared in these collisions, flashing into existence for perhaps a billionth of a second before recombining with the detector or decaying into other particles. These new particles that appeared were not pieces of a proton or neutron, but were created from the energy released by the collision according to Einstein's formula for the inter-conversion of mass and energy, $E = mc^2$. Theorists took a hint from Dmitri Mendeleyev's 1860's organization of the chemical elements into the Periodic Table and constructed a mathematical scheme to make sense of the menagerie of new particles.

Not everyone agreed with this approach. In the 1950s and 1960s physicists were used to the idea that protons and neutrons, the stuff of nuclei, were indivisible. Murray Gell-Mann, Feynman's office neighbor and collaborator on the weak interaction, was at the forefront of the move to systematize the particle families. Gell-Mann eventually won the Nobel Prize in 1969 for his classification scheme for elementary particles. He called these new fundamental particles quarks. At the beginning he believed them to only be mathematical toys that he needed to develop his theory and that they didn't really exist.

Feynman remained on the fringes of the controversy. The complex mathematics and logical arguments were not satisfying. He wanted to start from basic principles to build an explanation from the ground up. Feynman knew that Gell-Mann was working in the area, so even though their offices were close he purposely avoided talking to him about it. He read only enough to recognize that high energy physics was rapidly becoming disconnected from reality and then put away the articles. When asked why he hadn't taken part in the discussions he later told a historian, "I've always taken an attitude that I have only to explain the regularities of nature—I don't have to explain the methods of my friends."

In June 1968, Feynman began thinking about the protons and neutrons in the nucleus as made up of large numbers of small particles he called partons. For the simplest case he imagined what an electron would see as it raced toward a proton at a speed close to that of light. The effects of relativity described by Einstein would flatten the spherical proton, slowing time and thus the motion of the partons inside the proton. To the speeding electron a proton was a pancake in which point-like partons were embedded like blueberries. Feynman's idea was that when an electron or another proton collided with a proton, most of the point-like partons sailed on by the electron or each other, but sometimes the electron interacted with a parton, or two of the partons in the colliding protons interacted.

Feynman analyzed parton interactions using methods and diagrams adapted from those he invented for quantum electrodynamics twenty years earlier. It worked amazingly well. As a bonus, unlike the cumbersome mathematical theories of other physicists which considered each parton separately, Feynman's general method could handle many parton interactions at the same time by summing their interaction probabilities.

To test his new ideas, Feynman designed the simplest collision experiment. The Stanford Linear Accelerator Center (SLAC) had been built to fire a beam of electrons down a two-mile long tube into protons and observe the new

Aerial view of the two-mile long particle accelerator at the Stanford Linear Accelerator Center in California.

particles created. Conveniently, Feynman's sister Joan was living at the time right across from the accelerator. During the summer of 1968, Feynman visited Joan often, staying at her house during the accelerator runs and conferring with the resident SLAC experimenters about their most recent results.

He came across experiments run by Stanford physicist James D. Bjorken that were a suitable test of his method and thought he recognized some patterns in the data. After a feverish evening of calculation, Feynman found that Bjorken's observations supported his predictions. Bjorken had also analyzed his data, but he used the modern current algebra theory that most high energy physicists were using. His data fit the theory, but the complex mathematical arguments didn't provide a physical picture.

Feynman's explanation made immediate sense to Bjorken and the other experimentalists. They began to test his model with additional experiments that stretched the model and the results continued to support its generality. Feynman's indifference about publishing delayed his first parton paper until 1971, but nothing stopped him from talking about the ideas. Eventually, partons became synonymous with Gell-Mann's quarks and Feynman's terminology and reasoning permeated the field for a number of years. By that time, though, Feynman was ready to move on again. He complained, "This parton thing has been so successful that I have become fashionable. I have to find an unfashionable thing to do."

Gell-Mann had worked for years arranging the families of particles and developing the mathematical formalism that allowed him to postulate the existence of quarks. He was bitter over the rapid acceptance of Feynman's parton theory. The reason for the popularity of partons among physicists was that they opened an intuitive avenue in a field wallowing in elegant but abstract mathematics. Gell-Mann was only

Murray Gell-Mann (b. 1929), Feynman's colleague at Caltech, received the 1969 Nobel Prize in Physics for his theories about particles that make up atoms, which he called quarks. These are known as elementary particles, because they are not formed from smaller particles.

slightly mollified by receiving the 1969 Nobel Prize for his quark classification scheme.

The relationship between Feynman and Gell-Mann, the two Caltech Nobel laureates, had always been a strange one, even though Feynman was responsible for bringing Gell-Mann to Caltech back in 1954. Their styles were opposite from one another, mathematical versus intuitive, broadly educated versus deliberately uncultured. Yet, their physics fed off of one another. Their contrary approaches sought the common goal of explaining nature's innermost workings. Despite all of the conflict between the two premier physicists, real and imagined, it is suspected that it was Gell-Mann behind the scenes at Caltech who made sure that Feynman could pursue his own interests and could ignore grants and the other issues that trouble academic life.

Although the quark concept could be used to explain the general picture of high energy collisions of nuclei, no one had ever seen an isolated or bare quark. The reason for this was that the strong force was unlike other forces that grew weaker with distance. It was like stretching a rubber band, growing stronger the more the band is stretched. New quarks were created from this stretching energy provided by the collision when the "rubber band" broke. They combined rapidly in various quark pairs and triplets to form new particles called pions that were observable. Careful experiments from 1972 on at CERN in Switzerland revealed that jets of particles were formed rather than single particles.

Feynman and a postdoctoral student, Richard Field, worked on explaining the properties of the jets. To provide a real test of their theory they focused only on aspects that could be experimentally evaluated. In addition, Feynman insisted that they only predict the results of higher energy experiments that hadn't been performed yet. Their model went back to Feynman's roots in quantum electrodynamics

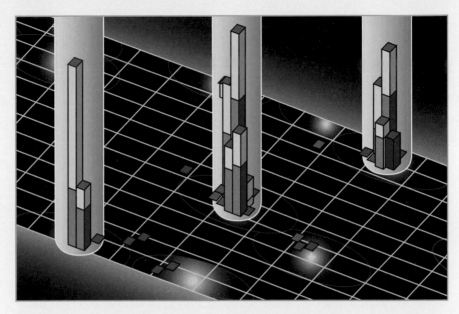

(Top) This illustration was created by scientists at Fermilab to represent data gathered from an experiment using the facility's Collider Detector, a particle accelerator. Physicists observed three energetic jets of particles, which they found are manifestations of the quarks and gluons that make up the proton. (Bottom) A facility at the European Organization for Nuclear Research, also known as CERN, where the first discovery of particle jets was made during the early 1970s.

(QED), substituting the language and rules of quantum chromodynamics (QCD) where quarks replaced electrons and gluons replaced the photon. The higher energy experiments confirmed their predictions. Although many details were still unresolved, Feynman was delighted with the success of QCD saying, "I am now a confirmed quarkanian."

With his fears of lack of creativity comfortably submerged beneath his successful parton and QCD work, Feynman allowed himself to slide more into the elder statesman-scientist role. He was more concerned than ever with the lack of rigor in education and in the reasoning ability of society in general. He impressed on the Caltech undergraduates at the 1974 commencement the importance of absolute integrity, in science and in life. "The first principle is that you must not fool yourself—and you are the easiest person to fool. So you have to have to be very careful about that."

Despite his difficulties in working with his own graduate students, Feynman was beloved by many students, even students of Gell-Mann, and to the young faculty in the department. Undergraduates were excited about the visual images he conveyed about physics. Post-graduates and faculty colleagues marveled at his energy and interest in every aspect of physics and his ability to untangle their thinking about any problem they were working on. One graduate student recalled, "Murray [Gell-Mann] was clever, but you always had the feeling that if you weren't so lazy and worked really hard, you could be just as clever as him. Nobody ever felt that way about Dick [Feynman]."

Outside his science career, Feynman continued to seek out interesting people. A few years after arriving at Caltech he met the Pasadena artist Jirayr Zorthian at a party and they soon became good friends. They were both freewheeling creators, even though one was logical to a fault while the other thrived on emotions and abstraction. The Feynmans bought a small house close to Zorthian's beach house and the two families enjoyed the beach while the children played. For a number of years they alternated Thanksgiving dinner at each other's houses in Pasadena.

Feynman and Zorthian had a long-running argument about beauty in art and science that was good-natured, but it bothered Feynman. Finally, Feynman decided that their arguments were because he didn't know anything about art and Zorthian didn't know anything about physics. They agreed that on alternate Sundays they would give lessons to each other on art or physics. Feynman had a special reason for learning to draw. "I wanted to convey an emotion I have about the beauty of the world. It's difficult to describe because it's an emotion." He wanted a way to communicate so that people other than physicists could understand the beauty that he saw.

Though Zorthian was unable to learn physics Feynman was determined to learn to draw. He worked hard, carrying around a pad of paper to practice his drawing. He took classes at the Pasadena Art Museum and began drawing from live models. As his work improved he found that he was developing his own style and began to appreciate the techniques of the great artists when he went to exhibitions that he had never been able to see before. Several of his drawings were displayed in a small art show and one of them sold. He wasn't interested in making money, but decided that if it made people happy to take his art home, he would sell it. However, he didn't want people buying his art because he was a physics professor so he made up a name, Ofey from the French "Au Fait," meaning all done, to sign his works. This mysterious unknown Ofey artist enjoyed a modest amount of interest on the Pasadena art scene. Zorthian and Feynman now had a new argument. Was Zorthian a better teacher than Feynman, or was Feynman a better student than Zorthian?

In the summer of 1977, while he and Gweneth were vacationing in their favorite place in the Swiss Alps, Feynman suddenly became violently sick to his stomach. He recovered quickly and made light of his experience so they could finish their vacation. Gweneth had just recently been treated for cancer and he didn't want to worry her. Back in Pasadena he was twice diagnosed with an unknown fever. Abdominal pain finally drove him into the UCLA Medical Center in October 1978, where they diagnosed and then successfully removed a six-pound football-size tumor from his abdomen. The tumor, a malignant myxoid liposarcoma, was an aggressive rare cancer of soft tissue and connective tissue. He had ignored the symptoms long enough for the tumor to destroy his left kidney and adrenal gland, as well as his spleen. Before the operation, Feynman asked his surgeon, Dr. Donald Morton, to restore him to consciousness if it looked like he wouldn't recover so he could "see what it was like to go out," rather than to die under anesthesia.

After the operation he talked to the physicians and then spent many hours in the medical library reading as much as he could about his cancer, much as he had done for Arline's tuberculosis thirty-six years earlier. He still didn't trust doctors until he checked the facts out himself. The reading brought him to the same conclusion as his physicians: he would be lucky to live ten years.

Feynman had always classified philosophy and psychiatry as soft subjects that masqueraded as serious fields of study. Philosophy seemed constantly shifting and there was no way of verifying its assumptions. His lack of respect for psychiatry stemmed from its use of medical language to hide what he saw as a lack of rigorous scientific proof. He considered his mind his private territory and wondered how someone could possibly judge him without knowing what he was thinking. A favorite story was of his experience during a postwar draft physical exam after he returned from Los Alamos of being rated 4-F, mentally deficient, by a military psychiatrist.

Feynman also had little positive to say about experimental psychology which he believed was sloppy reasoning dressed up with pseudoscientific language and methods. However, he loved the introspective side of psychology where he tried to figure things out about himself. As an MIT undergraduate he had tried to study how he fell asleep and experimented with manipulating his dreams. Now in his sixties he let his grey hair grow into a shaggy mane and began attending self-improvement seminars given by Werner Erhard on mystical world views. He also visited the sensory deprivation tanks of John Lilly, floating weightless in an Epsom salts bath in a dark soundproof chamber, hoping to have hallucinations. He practiced the methods of Baba Ram Das, formerly Richard Alpert of Harvard, trying to experience that cult leader's out-of-body experiences. Although his friends worried that he was trying to become a hippie, in practice he ignored all of the pseudoscientific mysticism, but he wanted to see how far his mind could take him— especially now that he was aware that death was hovering not far away and that his body was steadily failing.

Feynman was fifty-nine years old when his first paper on QCD was published. He had succeeded in demonstrating that although winning the Nobel Prize presented certain challenges to creativity, it did not necessarily end a career. In fact, QCD would be Feynman's last big effort in physics. However, it was not the end of his intellectual productivity. He realized that the future was closing in and he was determined to make the best use of the time he had left.

As he grew older, Feynman became interested in the so-called New Age Movement, a hodgepodge of spiritual beliefs taken from nontraditional sources and focused primarily on self-fulfillment. However, in his books Feynman commented that he found most New Age practices nonsensical, complaining that they often represented pseudoscience.

CHAPTER NINE

Fundamental Limits

While his two children were growing up, Feynman tried to stimulate their interest in a wide variety of subjects, just as his father had done for him and his sister. Unlike his father, though, he was careful not to push them only towards science, especially physics. He didn't care what Carl and Michelle decided to do in their careers as long as they were happy and good at what they did. He said, "I would be just as happy if they decided to be truck drivers or guitar players. In fact, I would even like it better if they went out in the world and did something real instead of being professors like me."

Still, Carl clearly had a technical bent, which his father was proud of and quietly encouraged. Michelle was more artistic. She was interested in art and photography and played the cello. He had a picture of Michelle playing her cello on his Caltech office wall. Feynman's only musical interest other than playing his bongos and listening to other percussion instruments was in hearing Michelle play.

Carl upset his father, though: when deciding on college, in spite of his technical interests, his first choice of a major was philosophy. Feynman commented in a letter to Carl: "After much effort at understanding I have gradually come to accept your decision to become a philosopher . . . I see you have chosen philosophy, over clear thought . . . so that you can fly above common sense to far higher and more beautiful aspects of the intellect. Well, it must be wonderful to be able to do that." Carl ended up enrolling at his father's alma mater, MIT, and soon switched to computer science.

While they were visiting MIT, Feynman introduced Carl to Marvin Minsky, one of the early workers on machine artificial intelligence. Carl wanted to do more than take classes and study, and through Minsky, Carl teamed up with Daniel Hillis, a graduate student whose thesis project was to build a computer fast enough to simulate common sense reasoning problems.

The computers of the 1980s were too slow and cumbersome to perform many tasks. Increased calculating speed was gained by clever programming and ingenuity in constructing the hardware. Hillis's idea was to radically transform both the way computer architecture was arranged, and the programming software for performing the calculations. His machine would be made up of many small computers that would each solve a small piece of a problem. The multiple answers would be passed on to another computer which would assemble the results into a solution, a concept called parallel processing.

The multiple processors idea fascinated Feynman. It reminded him of his days at Los Alamos when he was in charge of the Technical Computations Group and he organized the wives of scientists into teams plying calculators, and each team would compute a piece of the problem with different mathematical operations.

As the computer field developed, John Hopfield and some others at Caltech felt that a more extensive computer course was needed to broaden student interests and to solidify the presence of computer science at Caltech. They wanted to position their graduates to be leaders in the rapidly expanding computer industry. In early 1981, Hopfield and Carver Meade, another faculty member, approached Feynman with the idea to develop a course. He agreed to join them and the interdisciplinary course "The Physics of Computation" was scheduled for the fall term.

Since Hopfield, Meade, and Feynman weren't computer experts, they brought in several outside experts from the strong computer industry in Southern California to give lectures. Hopfield, Meade, or Feynman would then give a follow-up lecture to further develop significant points and fill in any gaps. It was a learn-as-you-go experience for all of them.

Although Feynman helped design the computer course, Hopfield and Meade ended up taking over the course the first year when he suffered the first recurrence of his abdominal cancer. In September 1981, physicians found that Feynman's abdominal tumor had reappeared, this time complicating surgery by wrapping itself firmly around his intestines. After chemotherapy and radiation failed to reduce the tumor mass, Feynman underwent fourteen and a half hours of surgery during which his aorta split. After an emergency call, more than one hundred students and staff from Caltech and the nearby Jet Propulsion Laboratory lined up to donate the seventy-eight pints of Type O blood that Feynman needed.

Feynman did not bounce back as fast as he had from his first operation. The rapid recurrence of the cancer compounded by high blood pressure and a heart arrhythmia were signs that he was living on borrowed time. Further heightening his sense of mortality, his eighty-six year-old mother Lucille died peacefully two days before this second operation.

As he slowly recovered from the operation he began to relax his guard on his time. He gave lectures on physics at the

Hughes Aircraft Company and consulted for them on a computing technique called neural networking while working on non-linear optical materials at the 3M Company. He spent more time on his drumming, his art, and his fascination with self-awareness.

His long-time drumming partner, Ralph Leighton, a local high school teacher and son of Caltech physicist Robert Leighton, aided and abetted him in numerous escapades. One of these was planning a trip to an obscure area of the Soviet Union, Tannu Tuva, that Feynman remembered from childhood stamp collecting. This quest, which was hindered by the mistrust between the USSR and the United States during the Cold War, occupied nearly ten years of arrangements.

By the fall of 1982, Feynman was still weak, but he felt well enough to teach. After the first year, Hopfield, Meade, and Feynman decided that they had learned enough to teach the computer course themselves. A stroke of luck brought one of Carl's teachers at MIT, Gerald Sussman, to Caltech for a sabbatical in 1983. Feynman hastened to talk with him. "My son says you're a pretty good teacher. I am going to teach a course on computing—on the ultimate physical limitations of computing, and on the computational

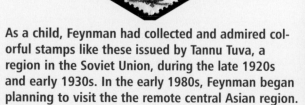

As a child, Feynman had collected and admired colorful stamps like these issued by Tannu Tuva, a region in the Soviet Union, during the late 1920s and early 1930s. In the early 1980s, Feynman began planning to visit the the remote central Asian region.

aspects of physics. Will you help me?" They struck a deal that Sussman would help if Feynman would eat lunch with him afterwards. Sussman said that it was the best deal he had ever made in his life.

While preparing for the computation lectures Feynman became interested in some of the fundamental questions about computation that were well beyond the mainstream use of computers. Did the laws of physics limit how small a computer could be and still perform calculations? Since reality was quantum mechanical, and computers were not, could a regular computer ever truly simulate the real world? The answer to the first question was that a single atom could be the smallest computer, encoding information in electronic spin states. The second question was more complicated. From the physics of the processes, he deduced that there was no minimum amount of energy needed to perform a calculation, so long as no information was destroyed in the process, which meant saving both the starting data and the calculated result. As computers became more ideal and smaller, less energy would be required to run them.

He published a conceptual model for a computer based on quantum mechanical principles and showed that it would not require energy input to perform a calculation and could simulate events at a quantum level. A functioning quantum computer has yet to be built, but some computer scientists such as Gerald J. Milburn feel that they are getting close. Feynman is often given credit for demonstrating the feasibility of quantum computing.

In the spring of 1983, Daniel Hillis, the graduate student that Carl had been working with to build a fast computer in the Artificial Intelligence Lab at MIT, was having lunch with Feynman. He said that he was leaving MIT to start a company to make a computer with a million parallel processors. Feynman responded "That is positively the dopiest idea I have ever heard."

Truthfully, though, Feynman was intrigued. He insisted that he spend the next several summers working at the company.

Feynman arrived at the old mansion house outside of Boston where the computer company was to be headquartered the day after the company was incorporated. Feynman promptly asked for his assignment. Startled because the co-founders were still trying to decide on a name for the company, Hillis chose the first problem he could think of and suggested that Feynman advise them on applications of parallel processing to scientific problems. But, Feynman didn't want to advise: "That sounds like a bunch of baloney. Give me something real to do." They sent him out to buy office supplies.

By the time he got back, Hillis and his colleagues decided that Feynman would be the best person to design the router, the heart of their computer that managed the communications among all of the different processors. They also had a company name, the Thinking Machines Corporation.

Feynman sat out in the woods behind the mansion, working out with pencil and paper what would happen with different router designs while everyone else at TMC finished getting the company set up. He loved the technical details and insisted on understanding what every instruction in the computer code did. When he wasn't working on a processing routine, Feynman could be found soldering a circuit board, stringing telephone or electrical building wiring, wielding a paintbrush, or showing a potential investor around the company and explaining what they were trying to do.

The camaraderie and sense of purpose at the Thinking Machines Corporation reminded him of Los Alamos, as did the young earnest faces. The only person with experience in managing a large project, Feynman could see that this group of idealistic but not-yet graduated scientists were struggling with the size and complexity of the undertaking. "We've got to get these guys organized," he told Hillis. "Let me tell you how we did it

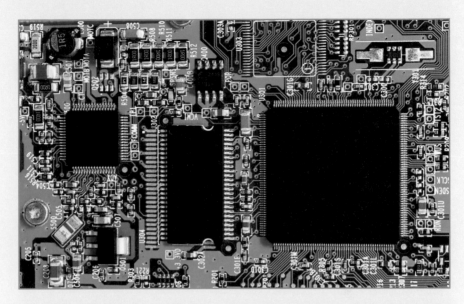

At MIT, Daniel Hillis had worked on making computers faster through parallel processing. Rather than asking a single computer processor to solve a large, difficult problem, Hillis found that the big problem could be broken down into smaller ones. Then, each of these problems could be assigned to its own computer processor, so that all could be solved simultaneously rather than sequentially. This would produce the solution in much less time. Feynman found the concept intriguing.

at Los Alamos." Feynman suggested that they pick an expert in each important area as group leader, an organizational feature that had spurred progress in Los Alamos. He also recommended inviting seminar speakers to suggest interesting uses for the parallel processing design, especially new applications that regular computers couldn't handle well.

By the time Feynman had worked out the router design they were already building a prototype which they named the Connection Machine. Their original goal of a million processors was too difficult to manage so they settled for 64,000 processors—sixteen processors per chip and 4,000 chips all wired together so that each processor could communicate with all of the others. A critical issue was the number of memory

The fifth and final version of the Thinking Machines Corporation "Connection Machine" supercomputer, known as the CM-5, was produced in 1991. This machine was used by the National Security Agency to break codes, and is now on display at the National Cryptologic Museum in Maryland. During the mid-1990s, Thinking Machines Corporation was absorbed by Sun Microsystems, which remains a major American computer company today.

storage buffers needed to prevent gridlock of messages exchanged between processors. They couldn't manufacture chips with the seven buffers each that would normally have been used. Feynman checked his calculations and said that five would be enough. The design worked, and the first program, Conway's Game of Life, ran successfully in April 1985.

Feynman worked at Thinking Machines off and on for almost five years. One benefit of working on one of the first supercomputers was that people were always bringing in new problems that had overwhelmed conventional computers. He spent most of the years after the first designs were launched working on a variety of computing-intensive applications which included analyzing images, reading insurance forms, geophysical models, protein folding, and database searching. He would ask for the simplest example to start with and then inquire how they would know that an answer was right.

Around this time, Feynman, considering his mortality, became interested in what kind of person he'd be remembered as. Hoping to improve and clarify his image, he began granting interviews. Charles Weiner, an MIT historian, conducted an in-depth series. Feynman also sat with other interviewers, and filled out a variety of psychological questionnaires probing the nature of creativity. Christopher Sykes filmed a series of interviews for the BBC, viewed on NOVA in the U.S., which became the program *The Pleasure of Finding Things Out* and later a book.

It was Ralph Leighton who crystallized the idea of a collecting Feynman's stories, which had been making the rounds of the physics community for years. During the 1980s, Leighton taped interviews with Feynman, then transcribed the stories and the two honed the tales for publication. Feynman insisted that this was not an autobiography, only anecdotes that he wanted to share. He chose the title *Surely You're Joking, Mr. Feynman!*, to poke fun at a remark made by the hostess at a Princeton social function when he had nervously asked for both milk and lemon in his tea.

W. W. Norton Publishers provided an unenthusiastic advance on royalties of $1,500 and the book appeared in a short print run in early 1985. To their surprise, *Surely You're Joking, Mr. Feynman!* required multiple printings and became a best seller, as did *What Do You Care What Other People Think?* published in October 1988 after Feynman's death.

Feynman's recurrent cancers concerned his sister Joan. She arranged with colleagues for a position at the Jet Propulsion laboratory and moved to Pasadena in the fall of 1984 to be near him. On Thursday nights she was a regular guest at the Feynman dinner table. They told stories about their youth, one of which recalled the time Feynman took her out to the Far Rockaway golf course to see the aurora borealis. Now there was a sequel.

After she had earned her Ph.D. in physics, Joan wanted to share her interest in the aurora with her brother, but she was afraid that he would solve all of the interesting physics before she got to it. They compromised. He could have the rest of the universe if he would leave the physics of the aurora to her. Later in the 1980s, while Feynman was visiting an aurora observatory in Alaska he was asked if he wanted to try to work out some of the puzzles of aurora physics. He replied, "I would like to, but I can't. I'd have to get my sister's permission." At a meeting of aurora experts later that year, Joan was asked whether her brother had been joking, to which she replied that the story was correct, he had asked her permission but she had turned him down. He left the aurora to her.

Feynman was not content to leave his life's work appreciated only by a small group of physicists. He wanted to be sure that his science could be understood by educated people, whatever their field of interest. From his struggles with the California educational system, he was aware of the growing gap between public understanding and the need for informed decisions that were required in an increasingly technological society.

He also wanted to finally be able to deliver on a pledge he had made. Over the years he had remained in touch with his high school friend Leonard Mautner from Far Rockaway with whom he had re-derived the rules of Euclidean geometry during one summer vacation and explored the world of chemistry. Mautner also had ended up in Pasadena, at UCLA. Mautner's wife, Alix, studied English literature but was interested in science. Often over the twenty-two years of their friendship she had asked Feynman to explain things to her. After his Nobel Prize she wanted to understand what he had done with quantum electrodynamics. He tried, but wasn't satisfied with his explanation. He promised Alix that he would prepare a series of lectures on QED for a popular audience that she could attend.

It took him longer than he expected. After trying out several approaches on different audiences at local colleges he finally felt he was ready. Unfortunately, in 1982, Alix died. Still, Feynman delivered on his promise in the fall of 1983 with a masterful explanation of QED in a series of four lectures at UCLA, dedicated to Alix. The lectures were given annually, and were transcribed and edited by Ralph Leighton. They were published in 1985 as *QED—The Strange Theory of Light and Matter*. These lectures were a crowning example of Feynman's skill in communicating difficult concepts to his audience.

Although he already had established his legacy in physics, there was still one more arena in which Richard Feynman had yet to perform. A cataclysmic series of events on a frigid morning in February 1986 set in motion the final triumph in Feynman's reputation as a great communicator.

In this closeup view of the *Challenger* lift-off, a cloud of grey-brown smoke can be seen on the right side of the solid rocket booster on a line directly across from the letter "U." To Feynman and other investigators who examined the evidence later, this photo provided the first visual sign that a seal in the rocket booster may have failed, leading to a catastrophic accident.

CHAPTER TEN

"I Believe This Has Some Significance"

The launch of the space shuttle *Challenger* on January 28, 1986, was the twenty-second in a series of missions for the spacecraft. The *Challenger*'s launch, STS-51 as the mission was called, was the first to include a civilian—teacher Christa McAuliffe—a testament to how safe the flights were believed to be. McAuliffe was to televise "Teacher in Space" programs in between the deliveries of two satellites into orbit.

STS-51 had already been postponed twice. Temperatures around Pad 39B at Cape Kennedy, Florida, dipped to twenty-eight degrees Fahrenheit, a potential risk for failure of the rubber O-rings sealing joints in the solid fuel booster rockets. Ultimately, the decision was made to go ahead with the launch. The flight lasted one minute and thirteen seconds until the main liquid hydrogen fuel tank exploded, sending the still firing booster rockets corkscrewing off to the sides and the capsule containing the crew plummeting into the Atlantic Ocean. An immediate investigation of the incident was ordered by President Ronald Reagan, including an independent panel convened to head off accusations of a NASA cover-up.

Several days after the accident, Feynman received a call from the head of NASA, William Graham. Graham had taken Feynman's Physics X course as a student at Caltech and had worked at Hughes Aircraft when Feynman was giving his noon-time lectures there. Graham asked him to serve on a Presidential Commission that would meet in Washington to review the evidence from the investigation of the explosion.

After Los Alamos, though, Feynman had sworn to avoid Washington, D.C., and anything that had to do with the federal government. Furthermore, it was not a good time for Feynman. After his second operation for his abdominal tumor, he had been diagnosed with a second rare form of cancer, Waldenström's macroglobulinemia, a blood cell disorder which put him at a high risk of a stroke or heart attack from overactive clotting of his blood. His initial response to Graham was a curt, "You're ruining my life," but he didn't tell him no.

Torn between what he knew was an important task and the realization that he might not live long enough to finish the investigation, Feynman asked several colleagues for their opinion. They told him that it was very important that he serve on the Commission. In desperation he turned to Gweneth, saying that this was a job that anyone could do and that they should get someone else. Gweneth told him, "No. If you don't do it there will be twelve people, all in a group, going from place to place together. If you join the commission, there will be eleven people—all in a group, going around from place to place together—while the twelfth one runs around all over the place, checking all sorts of unusual things. There probably won't be anything, but if there is, you'll find it. There isn't anyone else who can do that like you do."

Heeding Gweneth's advice, Feynman decided to participate in the investigation, but he made two conditions for himself. As

Members of the crew for Challenger's January 28, 1986, mission included (front, left to right) Mike Smith, mission commander Dick Scobee, Ron McNair (back) Ellison S. Onizuka, Sharon Christa McAuliffe, Greg Jarvis, and Judy Resnik. All seven members of the crew perished when Challenger exploded.

a partial compromise to his medical condition, after six months he would quit even if they were not finished. Second, during those six months he would do nothing else, devoting himself entirely to the investigation, seven days a week. It was the same way he approached problems in physics, with total commitment. He called Graham back. The next day NASA announced Feynman's appointment to the commission.

Once Feynman decided to join the investigation, he immediately got to work. He found someone to cover his teaching, and immediately plunged into his own investigation. One day before he had to be in Washington, he asked his former Ph.D. student Al Hibbs, head of the Jet Propulsion Laboratory (JPL) in Pasadena, to arrange for the shuttle program engineers there to brief him on the project. He spent the next day at JPL immersed in the technical details of the rocket motors, computers, and other shuttle systems.

A large piece of debris from *Challenger* is hoisted aboard a U.S. Coast Guard cutter. The navy and coast guard mounted a search-and-recovery effort to retrieve as much of the doomed shuttle as possible, so that investigators could figure out what had gone wrong on NASA's fifty-first shuttle mission.

The main concern of the engineers was material failure in the powerful main engines, which on previous flights had developed cracks in turbine blades. There were also reports from multiple missions of scorching of a set of rubber O-rings which sealed the joints between sections of the solid fuel rocket motor boosters, indicating that hot gases were leaking out of the joint.

After spending the day talking with the JPL engineers, Feynman took the overnight flight east to Washington for the first meeting of the Commission. He found that Washington did not operate with the intensity and single-minded purpose with which he approached his physics and had intended to pursue the investigation. There were many groups with a stake in the outcome of the inquiry, and everything was to be public. To give each faction a fair hearing required an organized, thorough progression of testimony. Feynman was impatient because his only concern was in finding out what caused the accident. He didn't worry about the consequences of the findings for organizations or for the future of the shuttle program.

Feynman was relieved that most of the Commission members had scientific training. Only the chairman, William P. Rogers, another lawyer, and an editor who would be writing the report did not have scientific backgrounds. At meetings, Feynman sat next to General Donald J. Kutyna, a former Air Force Space Shuttle Program Officer. The general quickly realized that Feynman would be extremely important to the investigation, and noting that Feynman wasn't used to the Washington way of doing things, he undertook to chaperone him through the process.

The crash had happened barely a week earlier so officials were still scrambling to complete the arrangements for the inquiry. William Rogers adjourned the first meeting shortly after scheduling a fact-finding trip to Cape Kennedy—five days later. Feynman was astounded. He had cancelled everything in his life to devote himself to the task of solving the mystery. Now they wanted him to do nothing for five days. He called Graham, the head of NASA, and said, "Listen, Bill. You got me into this; now you've gotta save me: I'm completely depressed; I can't stand it. I want to do something! I want to go around and talk to some engineers!" Graham promised to help Feynman go to Johnson Space Flight Center to talk to the engineers there.

Rogers balked at the idea. He was afraid that Commission members wandering around on their own would disrupt the delicate relations between NASA and other groups. As the chairman Rogers was responsible for coordinating a large number of activities and had to satisfy many groups of people with different agendas. The overall progress of the Commission would not be served by rushing ahead. Finally, he and Graham compromised by calling in several NASA experts to talk to Feynman.

One of the briefings the next day was on the seals in the solid fuel booster rocket, further confirming what Feynman had heard at JPL back in Pasadena. No one seemed to feel that this issue was particularly important. Feynman, though, felt that he was closing in on an answer and was disgusted that everything was moving so slowly. He was still in a bad mood the next day, a Sunday. Feynman went with Graham and his family to the Smithsonian Air and Space Museum for a special tour of the historical exhibits and a movie about the shuttle program.

Feynman had not paid much attention to the space effort during the 1960s and 1970s, but what he experienced at the Smithsonian convinced him that what NASA was trying to accomplish was worthwhile. Later that afternoon General Kutyna called Feynman from an Air Force Band concert and asked him what he thought cold would do to rubber O-rings.

William P. Rogers (center), the chairman of the Presidential Commission appointed to investigate the *Challenger* accident, arrives at the Kennedy Space Center for a briefing, February 1986. He is accompanied by the commission's executive director Alton Keel (left), and several aides.

Kutyna had been trying to find a way to pass along to the Commission concerns about the O-rings from a NASA astronaut whose career would be ruined if he went public.

On Monday morning, Feynman and Kutyna asked Graham for more information about the effect of cold on the seals, which Graham promised to get for them. That afternoon, a Morton-Thiokol engineer came uninvited to testify about the seals problem before a closed special meeting of the Commission. In addition, computer-enhanced images of the launch clearly showed puffs of black smoke and then a small flame spouting out of a test port in the direction of the shuttle's main hydrogen fuel tank. It was looking very much like they had found the culprit, but they needed the information on the resilience of the O-rings. When Graham brought them the reports, there was nothing about how the rubber would have behaved over the split second after the booster motor ignited. Feynman decided that the fastest way to find the answer was to do an experiment. The following day at a public meeting would be the soonest he could make his test.

Feynman stopped by a hardware store before the meeting to pick up a couple of screwdrivers, pliers, and a C-clamp. He pulled the sample of O-ring rubber from the NASA model of the booster rocket field joint in Bill Graham's office, and then sat next to General Kutyna in the meeting room to wait. He crimped the rubber in the clamp and slipped it into his Styrofoam cup of ice water. When he felt that the rubber was thoroughly chilled he reached for his microphone button. The general nudged him, "Copilot to pilot: Not now." The general jabbed a finger at a line in the briefing book to indicate when Feynman should make his point. When the speaker reached that slide Feynman activated his microphone and said, "I discovered that when you undo the clamp, the rubber doesn't spring back. . . . I believe that this has some significance for our problem." The TV lights and cameras turned on him. Holding the C-clamp, he unscrewed it, dropping the dripping ice-cold rubber strip on the table. The crimp in the cold rubber slowly straightened out. No one seemed to comprehend the implications of what he had just showed them. Then Rogers quickly said that they would consider that matter later, and adjourned the meeting for lunch.

While they were eating, news reporters asked Feynman about the putty in the solid booster field joint and to tell them what an O-ring was. He thought that he had failed to get his point across and was despondent. Later, though, from the reaction of the evening television news, it was clear that they had gotten his point, loud and clear. Amazingly, within the first week of the Commission's four month-long existence, thanks to Feynman's demonstration they already knew what had caused the accident.

Feynman spent two more months with the Commission collecting technical information and becoming more and more

Icicles hang from the service tower at Kennedy Space Center in Florida early on the morning of January 28, 1986. Unexpected freezing weather on the day of *Challenger*'s launch, beyond the tolerances for which the rocket booster's O-rings were approved, probably caused the rubber seals to fail. This allowed hot exhaust gases to leak under high pressure; like a welder's torch, the gas cut through the steel tank containing the rocket's highly volatile fuel, causing a massive explosion.

An interior view of the scorched hole in *Challenger*'s right solid rocket motor. The tapered edges along the hole indicate the inside-to-outside path of the fire that led to the explosion.

shocked by the lack of communication between the engineers who were warning about equipment stressed to near failure and management at NASA who were under pressure to keep the shuttle flying on schedule to retain their funding. The day before the Commission members were being flown to Kennedy Space Center to be briefed, he wrote to Gweneth, "I think it is possible that there are things in this that someone might be trying to discredit me if I get too close . . . My guess is that I will be allowed to do this overwhelmed with data and details, with the hope that so buried with all attention on technical details I can be occupied, so they have time to soften up dangerous witnesses, etc. But it won't work because (1) I do technical information exchange and understanding much faster than they imagine, and (2) I already smell certain rats that I will not forget because I just love the smell of rats for it is the spoor of exciting adventure."

When the rest of the Commission members went back to Washington, Feynman excused himself—against chairman Rogers' wishes— to do some exploring on his own. He ducked the management to talk directly with the technicians who refurbished the booster rockets after each flight. They were amazed that Feynman wanted to talk with them and not their bosses. He talked with the man who made the temperature measurements on the launch pad before takeoff. Feynman's unauthorized visits ended up saving face for Rogers. When Senator Hollings questioned the Commission's impartiality, the chairman was able to note that one of the Commission members, a Nobel Laureate, was at that moment investigating outside the official visit.

Over the next several months, as a member of the Accident Analysis Group, Feynman investigated the computer systems and the main engines. He was impressed with the computer systems even though they used obsolete technology because it had been proven reliable in the space program. The training of the flight crews also received high marks. He was fascinated by the contrast between how the engineers and NASA management each determined the risks for failure of critical parts of the shuttle. In his final report he was highly critical of management's willingness to lower standards of component performance despite warnings from engineers that recurrent design problems were not being fixed.

In April, when the Commission was preparing its conclusions, Feynman became embroiled in a dispute with Rogers about including his own report on the reliability of the shuttle in the official Commission document. He was afraid that the specific conclusions and recommendations that he had arrived at would be either lost or watered down in the consensus conclusions of the report. Feynman threatened to remove his name from the report. They compromised by including his private report as Appendix F which concluded with the statement, "For a successful technology, reality must take precedence over public relations, for Nature cannot be fooled."

Throughout the four months Feynman served on the shuttle Commission, he underwent tests to judge the state of his two cancers. In October 1986, back home in California, he underwent a third operation to remove more of the liposarcoma and cancer-riddled muscle tissue. He was able to bounce back from yet another major operation. "Another daring operation, another lease on life," he said. Feynman and his drumming partner Ralph Leighton continued to make plans to visit Tannu Tuva, a Soviet Socialist Republic outside of Outer Mongolia in Central Asia. The quest gave him something to look forward to.

In October 1987, Feynman underwent a fourth operation at the UCLA Medical Center. Doctors removed what they could of the abdominal tumor that had returned. This time Feynman did not bounce back rapidly. So much musculature had been removed that he found it difficult to stand upright. The *Los Angeles Times* prepared an advance copy of his obituary which he returned with the comment, "I have decided that it is not a very good idea for a man to read it ahead of time: It takes the element of surprise out of it." After several weeks he returned to teaching a graduate course in quantum chromodynamics, although he was clearly in a great deal of pain.

Feynman dealt with his impending death as matter-of-factly as he dealt with his science. It didn't scare him because he knew that death was an inevitable part of life. He didn't want other people to be sad about him dying. He tried to cheer up Dan Hillis who was distressed at losing his mentor and friend. "Yeah, it bugs me too [dying], but it doesn't bug me as much as you think it would, because I feel like I've told enough stories to other people, and enough of me is inside their minds. I've kind of spread me around all over the place. So I'm probably not going to go away completely when I'm dead!"

He began taking walks with Ralph Leighton to build up his strength for the Tuva adventure. On November 14, he participated in a panel discussion with a group of physics teachers at La Cañada High School on "What High School Physics Should

This building at Fermilab was named in Richard Feynman's memory. The Feynman Computer Center opened in 2001.

Include." Feynman grew animated, standing and gesturing, drawing energy from the questions posed by the audience. Talking about physics always excited him. It was his last public appearance.

On December 23, 1987, he called Jagdish Mehra, a physicist who was writing Feynman's scientific biography, to tell him that he was welcome to visit to finish up the book. When Mehra suggested early March, Feynman said, "I don't know. It might be too late then." Mehra flew out on January 9, 1988, and spent until January 27 taping their conversations. They took a break on Tuesdays and Thursdays mornings at ten while Feynman taught his quantum chromodynamics course. On February 1, 1988, Christopher Sykes filmed Feynman's last interview for the BBC.

Two days later Feynman entered the UCLA Medical Center. His abdominal cancer had returned, and this time it was inoperable. His one remaining kidney failed, and Feynman refused the dialysis that might prolong his life for a few extra weeks or months. Gweneth called his sister Joan and said "Richard says he wants to die, and that it's your decision." The two most influential women in Feynman's life met at the hospital and they went together to his room. They decided to honor his decision to not be put on dialysis.

He awaited the coma that follows kidney failure, attended by Gweneth, Joan, and his cousin Frances Lewine. Just before he slipped into the coma, Feynman apologized to Dr. Morton for dying on him. He wanted to observe his own death, like he had watched Arline die so many years ago, wondering if it would be the same. Until the end he was giving signals through the coma that he could hear and think. He would squeeze the person's hand he was holding. At one point he opened his eyes and said, "I'd hate to die twice. It's so boring," then slipped back under. At 10:34 PM on Monday, February 15, 1988, Richard Feynman died, three months short of his seventieth birthday.

The next day, Caltech students hung a banner from the eleven-story Millikan Library at Caltech, reading "WE LOVE YOU DICK." The memorial service on March 28, 1988, in the large Caltech Beckman auditorium had to be held twice to accommodate all of the well wishers. It was a fitting sendoff, a celebration of his life with a slide show, drumming, and brief remarks by friends and colleagues. A few days later, an invitation arrived from the president of the USSR Academy of Sciences to visit Tannu Tuva.

On December 31, 1989, Gweneth Feynman died of cancer. She was buried next to her late husband, under a simple flat pink marble headstone in Mountain View Cemetery in Altadena.

Danny Hillis missed Richard Feynman the most when he had something beautiful to explain, like a simple solution to what had been a very messy equation. Feynman loved those moments. When Feynman could transform the complicated into something simple, he felt that it was a sign that he was close to nature's secrets. One night Hillis dreamed that he had met Feynman and showed him a complex equation that reduced to $1/e^2$. He said, "Hey, Richard! How come you're talking to me? You're dead!" Feynman responded, "Oh well. At least we won't get interrupted this way!"

Timeline

1918: Born May 11 in Manhattan, New York City.

1935: Learns about Principle of Least Action from Abram Bader; graduates high school.

1939: Publishes first paper on cosmic rays; derives molecular force theorem (Hellman-Feynman Theorem) in senior thesis at MIT.

1941: Develops Wheeler-Feynman theorem of Action at a Distance; joins group working on uranium isotope separation after Japan attacks Pearl Harbor.

1942: Receives Ph.D.; marries Arline Greenbaum.

1943: Joins Theoretical Section in Los Alamos under Hans Bethe working on atom bomb.

1945: Arline dies; atom bomb successfully tested; leaves Los Alamos for Cornell.

1946: Father dies.

1947: Resolves to have fun with physics; applies path integrals to Dirac equation.

1948: Develops theory of positrons.

1949: Develops theory of quantum electrodynamics; diagrams accepted.

1950: Leaves Cornell for Caltech.

1951: Spends sabbatical year at the Center for Physics Research in Rio de Janeiro, Brazil.

1952: Publishes pseudoscalar meson theory; marries Mary Louise Bell.

1953: Studies phase transition in liquid helium; wins Albert Einstein award for QED.

1956: Divorces Mary Louise Bell.

1957: Discovers the theory of beta decay.

1959: Studies genetics on sabbatical.

1960: Marries Gweneth Howarth.

1961: Teaches freshman Lectures in Physics course.

1962: Son Carl born.

1964: Studies quantum gravity, polarons, and superconductivity.

1965: Wins Nobel Prize for QED.

1968: Adopts daughter Michelle; studies nuclear structure and theory of the nuclear strong force with Gell-Mann; studies quarks and partons.

1978: Diagnosed with cancer, a myeloid liposarcoma; operated on.

1981: Mother Lucille dies; has second operation to remove cancer; diagnosed with blood cell cancer.

1982: Teaches course on computing, theory of quantum mechanical computers.

1983: Begins work with Thinking Machines Corporation.

1984: Publishes *Surely You're Joking, Mr. Feynman!*

1986: Serves on *Challenger* Commission; undergoes third operation for cancer.

1988: Dies February 15; *What Do You Care What Other People Think?* published.

Source Notes

Chapter One: Far Rockaway

p. 9,   "I'm gonna commit suicide . . .", Richard Feynman, "Mr. Feynman goes to Washington," *Engineering and Science*, Fall 1987, 6-22.

p. 10, "If it's a boy . . ." Ibid., 12.

p. 12, "Mind the reasoning . . ." Jagdish Mehra, *The Beat of a Different Drum* (New York: Oxford University Press, 1994), 8.

p. 14, "You start at the beginning . . ." John Gribbin and Mary Gribbin, *Richard Feynman: A Life in Science* (New York: Dutton, 1997), 9.

p. 17, "He fixes radios by thinking." Richard Feynman, *Surely You're Joking Mr. Feynman!* (New York: W.W. Norton), 20.

Chapter Two: Budding Physicist

p. 20, "It was my only . . ." Mehra, *The Beat of a Different Drum*, 25.

p. 20, "mathematics and science were of . . ." Ibid., 27.

p. 25, "half a line," James Gleick, *Genius* (New York: Vintage Books, Random House, 1992), 86.

p. 25, "Why do you want . . ." Mehra, *The Beat of a Different Drum*, 79.

p. 26, "It seems that . . ." Gribbin and Gribbin, *Richard Feynman: A Life in Science*, 60.

Chapter Three: Project Y— Los Alamos

p. 29, "write up what you have . . ." Mehra, *The Beat of a Different Drum*, 140.

p. 32, "It was the first time . . ." Ibid., 152.

p. 36, "She's dead . . ." Ibid., 149.

p. 36, "a love like no other . . ." Feynman, *What Do You Care What Other People Think?* (New York: Bantam Books, 1989), 33.

p. 37, "The baby is expected." Gribbin and Gribbin, *Richard Feynman: A Life in Science*, 100.

p. 39, "A remotely located . . .." Robert S. Norris, *Racing for the Bomb* (South Royalton, VT: Steerforth Press, 2002), 407.

p. 39,   "It's a terrible thing . . ." Gleick, *Genius*, 133.

p. 40,   "Everything was perfect . . ." Michelle Feynman, *Perfectly Reasonable Deviations from the Beaten Track* (New York: Basic Books, 2005), 68.

Chapter Four: Adrift—Epiphany

p. 43,   "The dreams that I. . ." Gleick, *Genius*, 228.

p. 44,   "D'Arline, I adore you . . ." Ibid., 223.

p. 44,   "My darling wife, . . ." Ibid., 224.

p. 45,   "Feynman depressed . . ." Mehra, *The Beat of a Different Drum*, 172.

p. 46,   "That's all I'm going to do . . ." Ibid., 173.

p. 48,   "We need an intuitive leap . . ." Ibid., 226.

p. 49,   "I can do that . . ." Richard Feynman, "The Development of the Space-Time View of Quantum Electrodynamics," *Science*, 1966, 699.

p. 49,   "Finally he retired . . ." Mehra, *The Beat of a Different Drum*, 177.

p. 51,   "I had too much stuff . . ." Gleick, *Genius*, 258.

p. 52,   "nobody but Dick could use . . ." Gribbin and Gribbin, *Richard Feynman. A Life in Science*, 114-115.

p. 52,   "Well, Doc . . ."Gleick, *Genius*, 270.

Chapter Five: "There was a Moment When I Knew How Nature Works"

p. 56,   "I get so much fun . . ." Feynman, *Surely You're Joking, Mr. Feynman!*, 205.

p. 58,   "Someone who's wise . . ." Ibid., 205.

p. 59,   "Feynman had signed . . ." Gleick, *Genius*, 316.

p. 63,   "Won! Hot dog!" Mehra, *The Beat of a Different Drum*, 392.

p. 63,   "A man's generosity . . ." Ibid., 393.

p. 64,   "Townes and others who . . ." Ibid., 438.

p. 64,   "It was quite powerful . . ." Ibid., 436.

p. 66,   "Could it be . . ." Ibid., 462-463.

p. 67,   "No, what you mean . . ." Ibid., 464.

p. 67,   "There was a moment. . . ." Ibid., 338.

p. 67,   "I felt that I knew something. . ." Ibid., 467.

Chapter Six: Teacher

p. 71,   "I was overjoyed . . ." Michelle Feynman, *Perfectly Reasonable Deviations from the Beaten Track*, 103.

p. 74,   "I got a tremendous boost . . ." Mehra, *The Beat of a Different Drum*, 441.

p. 75,   "Anyone who had heard . . ." Ibid., 482.

p. 76,   "Look, why don't we get . . ." Ibid., 483.

p. 76,   "Look, Richard, you have spent . . ." Ibid.

p. 77,   "At the end of two years . . ." Ibid., 486-487.

p. 77,   "I've put a lot of energy . . ." Ibid., 588.

p. 78,   "I am inspired . . ." Ibid., 444-445.

p. 81,   "[Then] we compare . . ." Gribbin and Gribbin, *Richard Feynman. A Life in Science*, 178-179.

Chapter Seven: A Change in Perspective

p. 83,   "I don't feel . . ." Mehra, *The Beat of a Different Drum*, 570.

p. 84,   "Without using . . ." Gleick, *Genius*, 398.

p. 86,   "My desire to resign . . ." Ibid., 383.

p. 86,   "Professor Feynman?" Feynman, *Surely You're Joking, Mr. Feynman!*, 305.

p. 87,   "We have designed . . ." Gleick, *Genius*, 378.

p. 88,   "Listen, buddy . . ." Ibid., 378.

p. 89,   "One word of advice . . ." Michelle Feynman, *Perfectly Reasonable Deviations from the Beaten Track*, 159.

p. 90,   "I'd like to bring back . . ." Gribbin and Gribbin, *Richard Feynman. A Life in Science*, 182.

p. 91,   "Mr. Feynman will pay . . ." Mehra, *The Beat of a Different Drum*, 577.

p. 92,   "However, I remember . . ." Michelle Feynman, *Perfectly Reasonable Deviations from the Beaten Track*, 233.

p. 94,   "Don't let anybody criticize . . ." Ibid., 236-237.

p. 94,   "You know . . ." Gleick, *Genius*, 387.

p. 94,   "That's what I've forgotten," Ibid., 387

Chapter Eight: Nuclear Structure

p. 97,   "I've always taken . . ." Gleick, *Genius*, 391.

p. 99,   "This parton thing . . ." Ibid., 396.

p. 102, "I am now a confirmed . . ." Mehra, *The Beat of a Different Drum*, 523.

p. 102, "The first principle is . . ." Gribbin and Gribbin, *Richard Feynman. A Life in Science*, 196.

p. 102, "Murray [Gell-Mann] was clever . . ." Ibid., 215.

p. 103, "I wanted to convey . . ." Feynman, *Surely You're Joking, Mr. Feynman!*, 261.

p. 104, "see what it was like . . ."Gribbin and Gribbin, *Richard Feynman. A Life in Science*, 243.

Chapter Nine: Fundamental Limits

p. 107, "I would be just as happy . . ." Feynman, *What Do You Care What Other People Think?*, 100.

p. 108, "After much effort . . ." Gleick, *Genius*, 397-398.

p. 110, "My son says . . ." Anthony J. G. Hey, ed., *Feynman and Computation: Exploring the Limits of Computers*, (Reading, MA: Perseus Books, 1999), 45.

p. 111, "That is positively . . ." Ibid., 257.

p. 112, "That sounds like . . ." Ibid., 258.

p. 112, "We've got to get . . ." W. D. Hillis, "Richard Feynman and the Connection Machine," *Physics Today*, February 1989, 78.

p. 116, "I would like to . . ." Christopher Sykes, *No Ordinary Genius* (New York: W. W. Norton, 1995), 23-24.

Chapter Ten: "I believe this has some significance"

p. 120, "You're ruining my life," Gleick, *Genius*, 417.

p. 120, "No. If you don't do it . . ." Feynman, *What Do You Care What Other People Think?*, 117.

p. 123, "Listen, Bill . . ." Ibid., 130.

p. 125, "Copilot to pilot . . ." Ibid., 151.

p. 125, "I discovered that when . . ." Ibid., 151-153.

p. 127, "I think it is possible . . ." Ibid., 157.

p. 128, "For a successful technology . . ." Ibid., 237.

p. 129, "Another daring operation . . ." Mehra, *The Beat of a Different Drum*, 605.

p. 129, "I have decided . . ." Gleick, *Genius*, 437.

p. 129, "Yeah, it bugs me . . ." Sykes, *No Ordinary Genius*, 247.

p. 130, "I don't know . . ." Gribbin and Gribbin, *Richard Feynman. A Life in Science*, 256.

p. 130, "Richard says he . . ." Sykes, *No Ordinary Genius*, 253.

p. 131, "I'd hate to die twice . . ." Gleick, *Genius*, 438.

p. 131, "Hey, Richard . . ." Sykes, *No Ordinary Genius*, 255.

Bibliography

Brown, Laurie M., and Rigden, John S., eds. *Most of the Good Stuff: Memories of Richard Feynman.* Washington, DC: American Institute of Physics; 1995.

Feynman, Michelle. *The Art of Richard Phillips Feynman: Images by a curious character.* Basel, Switzerland: Gordon and Breach Publishing Group, 1995.

———, ed. *Perfectly Reasonable Deviations from the Beaten Path. The Letters of Richard P. Feynman.* New York, NY: Basic Books, Perseus Books Group; 2005.

Feynman, Richard P. *The Meaning of it All. Thoughts of a Citizen Scientist.* Reading, MA: Addison-Wesley, 1998.

———. "Mr. Feynman goes to Washington." *Engineering and Science* 51 (1986): 6-22.

———. Nobel Prize in Physics Award Address, "The Development of the Space-Time View of Quantum Electrodynamics." *Science* 153 (1966): 699-708.

———. *The Pleasure of Finding Things Out. The best short works of Richard P. Feynman.* New York, NY: Perseus Books, Basic Books, 1999.

———. "The problem of teaching physics in Latin America." *Engineering and Science* 28 (1963): 21-30.

———. *QED. The Strange Theory of Light and Matter.* Princeton, NJ: Princeton University Press, 1985.

———. *Surely You're Joking Mr. Feynman: Adventures of a Curious Character.* New York, NY: W. W. Norton and Co., 1985.

———. *What Do You Care What Other People Think?: Further Adventures of a Curious Character.* New York, NY: Bantam Doubleday Dell, 1989.

Feynman, Richard P., Ralph Leighton, and Alan Alda. *Classic Feynman: All the Adventures of a Curious Character.* New York, NY: W. W. Norton, 2005.

Feynman, Richard P., Fernando Morinigo, and William G. Wagner. *Feynman Lectures on Gravitation.* Reading, MA: Addison-Wesley Publishing Company, 1995.

Gleick, James. *Genius: The Life and Science of Richard Feynman.* New York: Vintage Books, 1992.

Gribbin, John, and Mary Gribbin. *Richard Feynman: A Life in Science.* New York, NY: Dutton, 1997.

Hey, Anthony J. G., ed. *Feynman and Computation. Exploring the Limits of Computers.* Reading, MA: Perseus Books, LLC; 1999.

Mehra, Jagdish. *The Beat of a Different Drum: The Life and Science of Richard Feynman.* New York, NY: Oxford University Press, 1994.

Milburn, Gerald J. *The Feynman Processor. Quantum Entanglement and the Computing Revolution.* New York: Basic Books, Perseus Publishers, 1998.

Mlodinow, Leonard. *Feynman's Rainbow. A Search for Beauty in Physics and in Life.* New York: Warner Books, Time-Life AOL, 2003.

Robbins, Jeffrey, ed. *The Pleasure of Finding Things Out. The Best Short Works of Richard P. Feynman.* Cambridge, MA: Perseus Publishing; 1999.

Schweber, Silvan S. *QED and the Men Who Made It: Dyson, Feynman, Schwinger, and Tomonaga.* Princeton, NJ: Princeton University Press, 1994.

Sykes, Christopher, ed. *No Ordinary Genius: The Illustrated Richard Feynman.* New York, NY: W.W. Norton and Company; 1994.

Wiener, Charles. *Oral Interviews with Richard P. Feynman.* Washington, DC: American Institute of Physics, 1966.

Web Sites

http://www.zyvex.com/nanotech/feynmanWeb.html

A transcript of Richard Feynman's classic talk, "There's Plenty of Room at the Bottom," is featured on this site. Feynman gave the speech on December 29, 1959, at the annual meeting of the American Physical Society at California Institute of Technology.

http://www.nobelprize.org/nobel_prizes/physics/laureates/ 1965/feynman-bio.html

Feynman's Nobel lecture, "The Development of the Space-Time View of Quantum Electrodynamics," which he gave on December 11, 1965, can be found here on the Web site of the Nobel Foundation, along with a brief biography of the Nobel laureate.

http://www.feynmanonline.com

A sampling of Feynman's art, his Lectures on Physics, and interviews with his friends, family, and admirers are available on this site. There's even an article and photo of Michelle Feynman, who realized her father's dream and visited Tuva in June 2009.

Index

Numbers in ***bold italics*** refer to captions.

Photo Credits

8: AP Photo/Dennis Cook; 11: Used under license from Shutterstock, Inc.; 12: National Archives &
Records Administration; 17: Used under license from Shutterstock, Inc.; 23: © iStockphoto.com/
Xin Zhu; 24 (both) Library of Congress; 27: Library of Congress; 30: U.S. Department of Energy;
33: U.S. Department of Energy; 34: U.S. Department of Energy; 37: U.S. Department of Energy;
38: Used under license from Shutterstock, Inc.; 39: U.S. Department of Energy; 40: U.S.
Department of Defense; 41: Library of Congress; 42: Used under license from Shutterstock, Inc.;
46: Fermilab Visual Media Services; 47: Science Source; 51: SPL/Photo Researchers, Inc.; 54: Estate
of Francis Bello/Photo Researchers, Inc.; 57: Photo by Manchete/Pictorial Parade/Getty Images;
58: Used under license from Shutterstock, Inc.; 61: Courtesy Cornell-LEPP; 64: Joe Munroe/Hulton
Archive/Getty Images; 70: Joe Munroe/Photo Researchers, Inc.; 73: Keystone/Getty Images;
74-75: Physics Today Collection/AIP/Photo Researchers, Inc.; 80: Library of Congress; 82: AP
Photo; 87: Used under license from Shutterstock, Inc.; 88 (top) SPL/Photo Researchers, Inc., (inset)
CERN/Photo Researchers, Inc.; 91: AP Photo; 92: CERN/Photo Researchers, Inc.; 93: Courtesy of the
National Library of Medicine; 98: Courtesy of SLAC National Accelerator Laboratory; 99: Physics
Today Collection/AIP/Photo Researchers, Inc.; 101 (top) Fermilab Visual Media Services, (bottom)
Used under license from Shutterstock, Inc.; 106: Fermilab Visual Media Services; 110: (both)
Private Collection; 113: Used under license from Shutterstock, Inc.; 114: Mark Pellegrini
(http://en.wikipedia.org/wiki/File:Thinking_Machines_Connection_Machine_CM-5_Frostburg_2.jpg);
118: National Aeronautics and Space Administration; 121: National Aeronautics and Space
Administration; 122: National Aeronautics and Space Administration; 124: National Aeronautics
and Space Administration; 126: National Aeronautics and Space Administration; 127: National
Aeronautics and Space Administration; 130: Courtesy Peter Ginter

Background interior and cover art by OTTN Publishing using artwork under license from Shutterstock,
Inc., and © 2009 Jupiterimages Corporation; Cover Image: Fermilab Visual Media Services